Women As Pastors

Ordained by God or Allowed By Man?

Dr. R. D. Anderson

iUniverse, Inc.
New York Bloomington

iUniverse books may be ordered through booksellers or by contacting:

iUniverse
1663 Liberty Drive
Bloomington, IN 47403
www.iuniverse.com
1-800-Authors (1-800-288-4677)

ISBN: 978-1-4401-5850-6 (sc)
ISBN: 978-1-4401-5849-0 (ebook)

Printed in the United States of America

iUniverse rev. date: 07/22/2009

All Scripture quotations are taken from the King James Version of the Bible.

Table of Contents

What's The Problem?

The church is the place where many people go to get an understanding of what their purpose in life may be. For me, one might say that I grew up in the church. My grandfather on my mother's side was a noted deacon in the church that my mother grew up attending. There are several men and women in my family that preach the gospel as licensed and ordained ministers. I myself have been a devoted and challenged messenger of the gospel for several years. After accepting my call to preach the gospel, I was encouraged by my pastor to attend seminary to better prepare myself to preach the gospel and better equip myself for my work in ministry.

It is understood that there are several controversial debates that take place with regards to the Christian church and the operation of the Christian church. Many of them have been debated and investigated for years and others for centuries. Many of the theories are based upon worldly beliefs, while others are grounded in biblical doctrine. In today's society there have been several, relatively new, controversial issues that have recently began to gain serious momentum and are quickly becoming the norm for what some people believe and consider to be biblically sound or based on a biblical foundation. Some people are hiding behind their own interpretations of the Bible and not the actual or literal meanings of the Bible. Others are just simply disregarding the Word of God to further their own agendas.

People are also trying to take what has been the traditional view of women, in the world, as the basis for why they are taking this opportunity to break out "against the establishment." There is a belief, by some, that there is some malicious chauvinistic view in the church to oppress women in the church. These ridiculous views are maintained as if the world were the one to have ordained the operation of the church. One of the many things that people [in the church] have to understand is that there is no "establishment" and the church only answers to Almighty God.

The Word of God is the most authoritative gift that we have been given and we must use it as our guide. The salvation of His children is at hand and most important for the leadership of His church. Everyone in the church is supposed to be working toward the same goal, and that goal is to reach all people with the gospel. We must all strive to reach that goal the way God has ordained and designed. In doing so, we should not be willing to risk losing even one soul, even if that soul may be your own.

As you read this book, it is my hope that you will realize that this book is not written to bash women. It is not written to sustain a questionable view of maintaining the oppression of women in the church. It is not even written to eliminate women from the beautiful task of 'preaching' the gospel. Moreover, it is written to bring all of us, in the church, in line with the same understanding.

I understand that it will be difficult for some people to let go of their opposing views. I also understand that there are some who will try to hold on to their view as a point of standing up for their personal beliefs. Some reasons for this may be that they founded or established a church that they are having great success at leading. There are others who may just refuse to be told what to do because they are just as capable at being a pastor as any man. Hopefully all of us will understand that being pastor does not come down to ability, capability or even training, it comes down to authority. Moses, by his own admission, lacked all of the ability to lead the children of God out of captivity. However, he had something that overcame his own view of himself and that was the authority of God. I am prayerful that pride will not be allowed to prevail where understanding has been given. After all, it is the Word of God that instructs believers to get understanding.

During my work towards my Masters and later my Doctorate degrees in Theology, the Holy Spirit inspired me to take a closer look at the subject of women pastors. Was it right, was it wrong, or was it a point that need not be reviewed because it was a subject that was not addressed in the bible? I worked long hours studying the subject, looking for books that covered the subject, attempting to understand what the real message from God might be. What I found was very little on the actual subject of women pastors. I was able to find a pamphlet here or a short paper there on the subject. I could find a few books with obscure passages that touch briefly on the subject, but I could not find any printed text that truly deals with the subject. Through my research and studies, I came to find that the Bible is the definitive source for real answers on the subject. Contrary to what some believe, the Bible clearly gives the church guidance on the subject. The guidance is not through any interpretation, misunderstanding, false messages or the like. It is in clear and precise words that all can understand.

Even with that, I was even more intrigued as to how a subject so big, so controversial has received such little coverage. Is it that people shy away from the subject? Is it that people do not want to draw attention to the subject? Or is it that text on the subject is just too hard to find because the message is hidden under an obscure title that makes finding the books written on the subject more difficult? Whatever the reason, this is as good a time as any other to bring light to the subject. I approached the subject hard from the middle and allowed the Holy Spirit to guide me to the left or right. Unfortunately, one cannot remain in the middle of the road on the subject once you gain an understanding of it.

In this day and time when we all need real answers to what God has said and what God has asked, how has this issue been allowed to slowly and quietly move to the forefront of church leadership? How is it that so many women have become pastors and the rest of the church remained silent? How is it that this has happened when God has conveyed to the church that His pastors "must" be men? There are several questions to be considered as you read this book to understand the conclusion of the matter. Can women teach the Word of God? Yes! Can women preach the Word of God? Yes! Can women lead the lost to Christ? Yes! Can women pastor God's Church? NO!

The above may be confusing to many. How is it that the answer can be 'yes' to the most of the questions and no to the last. If women can teach, preach, or lead the lost to Christ, then surely they can be pastors!

The answer is still no. Not because they are not smart enough, or wise enough or even strong enough. Not because they are not forceful enough, spiritual enough or even compassionate enough. It is "no" because God has clearly outlined the qualifications for His pastors in His Word which we call the Bible.

What Is Normally Understood?

> "That there should be no SCHISM in the body; but that the members should have the same care one for another" (1 Corinthians 12:25).

The issue of women pastoring is not necessarily a new concept; it just appears to be gaining an enormous amount of recognition in most recent history. The controversy stems from women speaking in church, in any capacity. A woman speaking in church has been an issue that has been debated, outlawed, banned, and eliminated from many churches throughout history. A woman speaking in church is not the issue that I am discussing in this book and I personally do not have a problem with that particular issue. However, it is difficult, to say the least, to discuss women being pastors without discussing the underlying issue.

I, in my travels, have seen several new churches sprout up in various places where a woman is identified as pastor, co-pastor or founder. There are fundamental problems with this phenomenon, notwithstanding that it goes directly and sharply against the Word of God.

Prior to the church's current understanding of the gospel and the message that Jesus Christ gave us; women were not allowed to preach at church in any capacity. We now understand that preaching by women was not forbidden, neither did God disallow it and though God may have left the door open with regards to women preaching in church this is completely and fundamentally different from serving as pastor of a congregation. And though it may be politically or socially acceptable, it is biblically unacceptable for women to hold the office of pastor in the church. This is not an opinion, not a chauvinist remark and not an attempt at maintaining a sign of power and superiority over women.

I understand that God left the door for women preaching open by giving us evidence in the Bible that women preached or ministered the word to others. Priscilla expounded the word more perfectly with her husband in Acts 18:25-26. In these verses we are told that "This man was instructed in the way of the Lord; and being fervent in the spirit, he spake and taught diligently the things of the Lord, knowing only the baptism of John. And he began to speak boldly in the synagogue: whom when Aquila and Priscilla had heard, they took him unto [them], and expounded unto him the way of God more perfectly."

The man that they taught the way of God more perfectly was Apollos, which the Bible calls "mighty in the scriptures" in Acts 18:24. Here we have a man who knew the scriptures still needing to be instructed in a better way to know God through a man and his wife. Both of them were there, in cooperation, to discuss the way of God to help him to be better.

Romans 10:14-15 tells the Bible reader that those who do not believe must hear the gospel to believe and to hear the gospel they need a preacher. The text does not say who the preacher should be, it does not say male or female, it does not say husband or wife. What it does say is that "they" will be sent. This is a clear representation of the fact that God did not close the door on women preaching the Word of God. Even at the most fundamental level, all believers should preach a message to at least one non-believer at some point in their life.

Preaching the gospel was not just left to men as many in the church still believe. It was left to all of God's people to seek the lost. If this particular task were left to just men, how is it that many women have done so much for advancing the Kingdom of God with their witness? Even those that have not exalted themselves to the office of pastor have done great things to advance their local churches and their local ministries.

We know that women serving as pastor is biblically unacceptable because God has been clear in his word. Some Bible scholars and some pastors would have the world believe that God has changed and is not the same as He has always been. But we know that God has not changed, and there are no biblical precedents to support a woman holding the office of pastor. I understand that many proponents of women pastors claim that there are no scriptures that say they should not be pastors. This is untrue, the office is clearly established through scripture and the occupants of the office are clearly identified.

The controversy comes about when people attempt to interpret the foundational scriptures that establish how the church should conduct itself with regard to women in service in the church. No, women are not relegated to just holding positions in the kitchen or on the hospitality board or even the nurses guild. You probably already know that there are many things that women can and are qualified to do in the church. However, each position in the church has a purpose and should fall within the scriptural boundaries of the Bible. This is especially true when it applies to church leadership with regard to spiritual direction.

I understand that some people will say that not all of the positions in church today are found in scripture. Where do you find trustees, or the nurse's guild or even youth leadership? Those that are so enlightened understand that God has provided a certain amount of latitude when it comes to managing the church operations. Many of us now understand that a greater impact can be made on youths if they are allowed to learn about the Lord and Christian living in a way that interests them.

Many of us now understand that various media outlets are available for evangelism. Many of us now understand that someone must maintain the supplies used in the church. These were all things that are not discussed in the Bible but we understand that doing the things necessary to manage them should not be hindered in any way. This is yet another difference to the Bible's applicability to the leadership in the church.

It is true that God would have us to reach as many people as we can and as many as we were created to reach. What is not true is that we do so by any means necessary. We, the church, present a picture of hypocrisy when in one instance we say that we preach the Word of God wholly and completely yet we avoid the scriptures that do not help our cause or our ideology.

If a pastor is an adulterer, will he preach against adultery, for it, or not at all? If a pastor is a thief, will he preach against stealing, for it, or not at all? If a pastor is a killer, will he preach against it, for it, or not at all? In this case, if a pastor is a woman, will she preach for it, against it, or not at all?

In either instance, with either issue, the dilemma remains the same. This is true whether the person commits one, none, or all three instances. He or she would still be wrong because he or she is become as a hypocrite. Furthermore, it places the preacher at a serious crossroads if any issue that goes against God's will is not properly addressed..

If the thief preaches that stealing is good or okay, it is obviously against the Word of God that clearly states that you should not steal. If he preaches against stealing he is obviously going against his own practice and therefore a hypocrite. If he avoids it all together he is a deceiver because he chooses to avoid exposing himself and his abandonment of following the Word of God or holding himself accountable to the Word of God. Either way the damage can be irreparable unless the person changes in one way or another. The easiest way to get on track would be to discontinue from the practice that does not line up with the Word of God and preach the word as God has delivered it to all of us.

The same holds true for the killer, the adulterer and the female pastor or bishop. Before the conclusion can be drawn that I am comparing females who hold the office of pastor to thieves, murderers and adulterers, I will say that I am not. What I am attempting to do is illustrate the fact that if anything goes against the Word of God, it is a sin. No sin is greater than any other sin. So this means that we should change from willfully sinning. This is especially important when we have been awakened or enlightened to the truth of a matter.

After enlightenment, the only thing that can keep a person from doing differently is his or her own pride. Bible scholars understand what the Bible says about the king of the children of pride (See Job 41).

Traditions tend to build a certain level of pride. Traditions are, unfortunately, what many people base their religion on. Fortunately, I do not have that particular hang-up. Though I grew up going to Baptist churches, and though I came to understand that women should not be preachers, I now know differently. This is not because of any particular teaching but because I want to teach what God's Word teaches, not my own beliefs. I have not been indoctrinated by traditional views, though I have been exposed to many traditional beliefs.

I cannot say that I ever remember a time were the subject of women preaching was ever taught to me as a practice to endorse or a practice to avoid. I do not remember a message, a bible study or even a vacation bible school where it was taught. Likewise, I do not ever remember seeing a woman preacher until I found out that my Aunt was a preacher. Though I was a little confused when I found out, it did not affect me much at all. I cannot remember the subject ever being openly discussed, by anyone, in the churches I have attended, but somehow I learned that a woman preaching was not an accepted practice. Maybe it was a subject discussed at home, at which I overheard a discussion and formed my view from what I heard. Or maybe a preacher, briefly, touched on it in the middle of another sermon to keep from being blunt about the subject and offending the women of the church. As I have grown older I have grown to form my understanding of various subjects not from what others may view as good or proper but by contrasting and combining my understanding of the scriptures with other's understandings and drawing, what I feel is, a sound conclusion of the subject.

Of course, this subject will be just as heartfelt on both sides as the subject of Eternal Security. People get heated when discussing that particular subject. I have seen people, who call themselves Christians, get mad or upset when standing in disagreement over that particular subject. The subject of women pastors is no different in some cases. People tend to believe with their heart on a particular subject matter. To challenge what a person feels may, at times for that individual, feel like a threat on that person's life. This is because it diminishes or kills something about who they are or what they feel. It, in a way, kills a portion of their personal history that they hold dear. It erases some of what makes us who we are when someone closes the book on something that we believe. This is one reason that many people find it so difficult to change.

What Christians must understand is that we stand in the midst of bringing the rest of the world together and into the knowledge and understanding of who Jesus Christ was, is, and shall be for all of us. If we are to disagree, we must do so with love and a heart of peace. We should not be so willing to express hate, disdain, or even dislike towards our brother or sister that stands on the opposite side of this particular issue. The desire is that eyes will be opened to look at the scriptures draw a sound understanding of what God's desire is for his people. We must cease from attempting to transform a few scriptures into a platform for what we may want to do.

Some may say that my view is my opinion or my belief. To them I say that if there is any fault, it should be found in the Word of God. I am but a messenger that has been led to submit this book into your conscious, how you chose to proceed is up to you. I understand that many will continue to search for ways to justify their particular position but I have found that sometimes it is easier to accept the truth. Truth is necessary for all of us to do this work to the best of our abilities. Without the truth we fail.

People do hold to some scriptural references for the basis of the traditional belief that women were to never speak in church. To the church at Corinth, The Apostle Paul wrote these words: "Let your women keep silence in the churches: for it is not permitted unto them to speak; but they are commanded to be under obedience, as also saith the law" (1 Corinthians 14:34).

These are some very strong words from the apostle. There is no debating what the scripture absolutely implies. However, is it written to be a standard practice for the church or is it written for another purpose altogether? If one were to study the issues and activities of the period in which Paul writes, one would see that there were many problems that arose in the various early churches that had been established. Furthermore, one only needs to look at the 1st Corinthian epistle to see this fact.

It is my understanding, through my studies, that when Paul wrote this epistle, he was dealing with certain nuances within the church. One thing that must be kept in mind when reading the works of Paul is that most of his writings reflect his mission to establish churches in the various places. His was an obvious calling to establish, or re-establish order in the churches of the day. As part of his mission to establish churches, he of course, had to groom or provide some direction for the church leadership. This is why many of the books he authored are known as the "pastoral epistles."

Many of his works were written as a guide for the establishing of the church and the behavior, characteristics, and strength of the leadership. As we look at his writings today we see that they were not written as just something that people could look at and say "that just applied to the church during Paul's time." Paul indeed wrote for the establishment of the church but he also wrote for the future benefit of the church today.

At this particular point Paul is writing to the church at Corinth in response to some bad reports he had received about "contentions" among the Christian brethren in Corinth. This is evidenced in the opening to this letter in the very first chapter (1 Corinthians 1:11). Paul received this report from members of the house of Chloe. One of the contentions was obviously with regards to women speaking in church. It is easy to make this conclusion because Paul makes it a point to discuss this particular issue within the body of the first Corinthian letter. He does not sneak it in as an afterthought; he establishes its importance boldly.

Obviously, from the scriptures it can be seen that some of the confusion in the early church arose in part from something that was happening with the women in the church. It was bad enough to Paul for him to make it necessary, for the church in Corinth, to command that the women be silent in their churches. The issue was not discussed in such a way in any of the letters to the churches in Galatia, Rome, Philippi, Thessalonica or Ephesus.

Some may say that it was not discussed because it had already been addressed in Corinth. However, I believe that it was not discussed because it was not such an issue for these other locations. Therefore Paul did not have to incorporate such an injunction upon those establishments.

This, however, is somewhat where the origin for the ban on women speaking in church stems from. However, was this command applicable to all churches from then on or just the church in Corinth? On the other hand, could this have been an early indication, by Paul, of what may be necessary for the maintenance of order in regular church services then and now?

I believe that people want to believe in God but they want to believe in him in their own way. This is why when we look out amongst churches today we see things that are contrary to the word of God taking place in the church. For instance, some churches are performing homosexual unions, some churches have openly gay ministers, others have privately gay ministers and some churches have women pastors and deacons. All of these issues are discussed in the Bible clearly and they are all being disregarded as if parts of the Bible do not apply or God has changed his position on them.

In principle and merit, a Christian's faith is built upon the complete infallible word of God. By sheer essence of those beliefs we are to take God at his word as it is written. To do otherwise is to discount the faith or in other words to show that we do not believe. When that becomes the case, then the Word of God is of no effect to us at all. A good way to look at the situation is to imagine a strong chain that is connected to itself at the ends. The chain has several links that connect it. It is complete and strongest with each link interconnected. Now picture someone cutting or breaking a link. Now the chain is different in several ways but most importantly, it is shorter and weaker because the broken link cannot be replaced and allow for the chain to provide the same level of strength and stability it had prior to its weakening.

The chain, in this example, would be the Word of God; the links would be the scriptures that make up the entire text. If we are allowed to take out scriptures that we do not like or that do not help our cause, then the rest of the Bible, like the broken chain, is of no use to us as God has meant for it to be.

It is clear that men and women both play valuable roles in Kingdom building. However, if we operate outside of roles for which the Bible has ordained we are, in essence and deed operating in a rebellious state to God. The word of God is even clear to point out that rebellion is much like another sin.

> "For rebellion is as the sin of WITCHCRAFT, and stubbornness is as iniquity and idolatry. Because thou hast rejected the word of the LORD, he hath also rejected thee from being king" (1 Samuel 15:23).

Rejecting the word of God is a sign of rebellion that appears to be at the center of the issue of women being pastor. By definition, it will be clear from the word of God that those women that choose to accept or initiate leadership positions in the church such as pastor or deacon are openly sinning. And by nature of their sin they are wrong because God's commandments are the church's law. Not only did Jesus tell Peter to feed his sheep, but he also commanded him to keep God's commandments.

Should She Keep Quiet?

As we try to gain an understanding of what would be the real truth behind whether women should be pastor or not, we have to explore the biblical text that gives us the answers to what we should follow and believe. Different scholars assert that during the time of the letters to Timothy there became a rise in the questions concerning the order of church service but in his letters to the churches, Paul attempted to deal with different issues that would arise in the different regions he visited. A great controversy is addressed in Paul's day and created in ours in which Paul declares: "Let your women keep silence in the churches: for it is not permitted unto them to speak; but they are commanded to be under obedience, as also saith the law" (1 Corinthians 14:34).

In his choice selection and use of words, Paul was not making a statement of command for a universally accepted behavior for all women in the church. Paul was making a declaration for the behavior of women in the church at Corinth. What is clear from his message is that Paul preferred that women kept silent in the Corinthian church in adherence to the law. Women apparently were a part of some confusion that was being experienced during the time of his letter because he makes this declaration after declaring that God is not the author of confusion as was the present situation in the church at Corinth.

It is indeed confusing for the church when God clearly gives the order of man in relation to God and women in relation to men through the Words of God.

Paul's discussion of women being silent is separate and distinctly different from his discussion of women in his 1st epistle to Timothy:

> "Let the woman learn in silence with all subjection. But I suffer not a woman to teach, nor to usurp authority over the man, but to be in silence. For Adam was first formed, then Eve. And Adam was not deceived, but the woman being deceived was in the transgression" (1 Timothy 2:11-14).

As Paul used the term "suffer" in the text he is referring to his personal desire to not permit women to teach or speak in the church. Paul's decision to say it this way, to me, is a clear indication of his intent. Though many may use this text as the basis for excluding women from ministry and not acknowledging women in ministry, this appears to not have been his exclusive intent. It is clear that Paul does not instruct Timothy to adhere to this practice. Paul does not here or anywhere else declare that this must be a standard for the operation of the church or even a practice that should be considered for adoption. For the sake of argument, neither does he discourage taking up the practice for managing the operation of the church.

Clearly, Paul writes this to illustrate and make known what had been his standard practice. He also writes this to illustrate what happened to be his preference for women in the church. However, he chooses not to venture any further than identifying what he practiced. Paul goes on to give adequate justification for following the practice by showing the weakness of the woman in referring to Eve's weakness in the Garden of Eden. He substantiates his position by making known the woman's tendency to be deceived as a core flaw of the woman. As Adam and Eve were in the garden, it was Eve who declared that she had been deceived by the serpent and she, in turn, misled her husband.

While all of us have or may have the capacity to be deceived, Paul is asserting that women were or are more easily deceived. How this relates to how women may operate in the church is unclear. However, the implication is that women could be deceived and thereby would allow their deception to become a part of their teaching. Or else, God forbid, they allow their deception to be used to mislead others as was the case with Eve and Adam. This could also be misused if they had authority over men. Nevertheless, for some, this is proof enough that God does not desire that women preach or teach at any time. This is no more true than if any pastor today established a rule for the operation of the church that he pastors and saying that all churches should follow that rule.

For example, many pastors have established rules for the occupancy of the pulpit. That is, they only allow certain people to enter, occupy or in some cases even clean the pulpit. However, not all churches adhere to those established rules nor are the churches that do not follow these rules in any particular violation for not following the rule. These are rules that pastors establish for the orderly conduction of service in their particular congregations. Paul understood, as many pastors today understand, that each church operates under rules necessary for the people of that particular church. Even churches under the same denominations today are not identical in how they are operated by the respective sitting pastors.

It is understood that many denominations were birth out of a group's or an individual's desire to not adhere to what was happening at a church that they were a part of initially. Some churches were birth out of a person's disagreement with the leader whom they were under and that person felt moved or was rebellious enough to desire to do things their way or, more hopefully, God's way.

What Paul has illustrated to us in 1 Timothy 2:12 is the fact that each leader of a congregation may need to administer some rules specific to that particular congregation for the orderly conduction of service. Anything that does not provide for the orderly conduct of service will have to be managed or eliminated. This is what Paul did when addressing the Corinthians. In his first epistle to the Corinthians 34:14, Paul commands the men to have their women be quiet in the church. He also told them that their women did not have permission to speak. In the latter part of the verse, Paul verifies his command by saying that the women were "commanded" to be under obedience as the law demanded. This is vastly different from what Paul told Timothy as a young pastor conducting church service.

What Paul told Timothy was, once again, what his standard practice happened to be for the situation that was at issue. The way that Paul delivers the message to Timothy was not as a command or even a strong suggestion. He gave it as a statement of fact. For Paul to make it a commandment, he would have had to word his statement differently. His statement would have had to have more of the command words such as commanded, shall, must, will, will not, shall not, do, do not, and go, etc. In essence, commands require the one receiving the command to do this or to do that. This is what Paul did to the church at Corinth. To the church at Corinth, the women were commanded to be under obedience. There was no such command given to his young student.

It must be pointed out that Paul's instructions concerning the silence of women were presented more as an alternative to something else. Paul could have told the men to leave their wives at home and tell them what they learned but he did not. It is clear, from earlier verses in the first Corinthian letter, that there was some sort of chaos occurring in the early church. This chaos was causing much strife in the church and it is possible that Paul was offering to the men a way to release some of the contentions by having the women keep silent during the service.

The silence commanded by Paul was not for all time. It was for the correction of an issue occurring at that time. It was presented for correcting an issue that the men of the period were obviously having significant difficultly dealing with on their own. Paul asserted his authority in his letter to relieve a troubling situation. Paul's discussion of what "he" does not allow women to do can be compared to his definitive description of the qualifications one must meet if one desires the office of bishop.

Another important point to be made is that Paul, in his letter to the young pastor, says to "let" the women learn in silence. This does not address preaching, but it does lend to the understanding that one will learn more if one listens more. I can remember as a young man, when I would do homework with the television or radio on my mother would come in and tell me to turn them off. Apparently, you are not supposed to study with noise in the background. It was not a problem for me, but I had to listen to my mother and turn them off.

It appears to be clear that there is no limitation on women preaching or speaking in church in totality. In fact, all Christians are expected to teach the word of God to others and reach all for God. I clearly see that women can be used mightily in this capacity. It is clear because the same Paul that commanded the women to keep silent in obedience to the law also called Christ of no effect to those who are "justified by the law." In these words, Paul explains that if you are to adhere to the law you must adhere to all of it.

Could It Be A Calling For Anyone?

"Let every man abide in the same calling wherein he was called" (1 Corinthians 7:20).

The controversy over whether a woman can serve as pastor is not limited to any particular denomination. The issue has plagued the church for many years. Under normal circumstances, a thorough history of the subject might be necessary. However, since this is being examined solely from a biblical perspective, the history of the issue is less important. The history is based more in traditional belief and less on biblical principal.

In our personal lives, most of us have some persistent issues that if left untreated they grow into problems that are more serious. In this case, the persistent issue has become women that desire the office of pastor. This desire could be a genuine feeling within the individual that they are "called" to the position, or it could be a combination of outward influences leading to the belief that it is their calling. I am one that believes 100 percent in a person walking or operating within their calling. However, I also believe 100 percent that your calling will fall in line with the word of God.

The belief that something is one's calling is not substantiated until it is confirmed by the Holy Spirit. That confirmation does not come from the ability to do it alone, it also comes from the allowance, appointment, and permission to do it. For God, He is not seeking individuals that secretly or even publicly invalidate what has already been written in the Bible. The Bible is God's authority to man and cannot be changed by men to accommodate chosen practices but should be used to verify their practices.

I believe some people in the church confuse their ability to do something with a calling to do something. On the other hand, some may make their dissatisfaction with how others operate in a position as confirmation of their calling to do better in that position. Oftentimes some may see other pastors in position and to them they appear to be ineffective and because they appear this way, to those individuals, they began to believe they could do a much better job in the same position. It is not necessarily bad to evaluate someone in the same position or profession as yourself. Evaluating others is oftentimes necessary for us to evaluate ourselves adequately. However, how we evaluate others is the same way that others will evaluate us. One person's shortcomings may be another's high points.

What must be held in high regard is that each of us is called to a particular position for a particular time and a particular purpose. When I look at my ministerial development, I realize that I was supposed to be an Associate Minister before I became a Senior Associate Pastor before I became a Pastor. It was the necessary order of things for my life and my spiritual development. God ordained each position and my spiritual maturity grew in each position. I would not be as effective a leader had I not gone through the growth process that God set for me, not to mention that I am still in the midst of this growth process. Likewise, I understand my calling to pastor better after having grown the way I did. If my calling were not to pastor, I believe that I would be just as effective and just as encouraged in whatever position, because I was called.

As it relates to calling, I first knew about my calling to preach at the mischievous age of 18. However, I did not accept that calling until I was 28 years old. During that 10-year span, I remember having at least five people tell me that I looked like I should be a preacher. Yet I was not particularly acting like a preacher so I did not take this as confirmation to my calling. No, my confirmation came when I sincerely sat down and asked God to make his desire for my life plain and clear. I remember the Holy Spirit clearly telling me to read a particular book in the Bible that spoke clearly to me, and I accepted my calling that night. Even still, I did not receive my confirmation to pastor until after I had accepted my calling to preach. Though many people may tell you that you should be doing something the real confirmation comes from within and from the Holy Spirit. Nevertheless, be clear and ever mindful that whatever it may be, will never contradict or nullify what is already written.

Some people try to show that God's word has some ambiguities in it that allow for interpretation on various subjects. Does this ambiguity also exist when it comes to the subject of women pastors, or are people out of line when choosing to go against what God has ordained?

Working for the Lord is a beautiful mission but it is even more rewarding when we move in the way that the Lord has designed. Moving outside of the Lord's design creates chaos and confusion in the church. This in turn reflects on the church in the world and then, the church bears no contrast with the rest of the world in regards to chaos and confusion. To eliminate this confusion we all must operate in the positions to which we are called even if it may not be the position that we want and even if we think we are capable of operating or even succeeding in a greater position.

Leadership is by design or divine appointment and not by desire in the church. Churches that were to seek a pastor were warned to not seek a pastor that was a novice. The consequence for seeking such a person is the possibility of that person being overcome with the pride of having the position and the one chosen can fall to the same condemnation of the devil (paraphrased 1Timothy 3:6). From this, we can see that the church, itself, has a responsibility to protect their pastoral choice from falling into the same fate of the devil. Would this not hold true for the church that was following the misplaced leader. I say misplaced because I want to be clear that there is a place for women ministers and preachers in the church. That place is clearly not the office of pastor.

While one must trust and believe in their calling, one must also qualify and verify one's calling. The Holy Spirit is clearly capable of doing whatever He so pleases however; the Holy Spirit operates within His own confines or his own area of responsibility. God's decision is not man's permission to do whatever he would like.

The calling to pastor can be considered a true gift of God. This is because it is a beautiful thing to have the opportunity to lead anyone to Christ. The following words are recorded in the book of Romans;

> "How then shall they call on him in whom they have not believed? and how shall they believe in him of whom they have not heard? and how shall they hear without a preacher? And how shall they preach, except they be sent? as it is written, How beautiful are the feet of them that preach the gospel of peace, and bring glad tidings of good things" (Romans 10:14-15)!

This, to me, describes the joy that should accompany the calling to preach. That joy is increased in a person's calling to pastor, if the called truly work to please God. That is the beauty in the calling to pastor because you are sent to deliver the word of

God. Once again, all preachers are not pastors though all pastors should be preachers. Pastors are not supposed to serve their own agendas when it comes to matters involving the church. Instead, we are challenged to serve God and man. We serve God by adhering to His word and man by bringing them into an understanding of God in addition to ministry and helping our brothers and sisters. If what we do takes the focus off of God or detracts from the word of God, then we as ministers, preachers and pastors are the ones that are wrong.

For instance, I myself was one who had to make a choice to remove anything that would detract from God's word and put people's focus on me. When I was younger, I became a member of a well-known and well-storied organization. As such, I later found that people had horrible and devilish views of the organization and the background of the group. In fact, some viewed it as a group with a history of pagan worshippers. Although I never participated in such activity nor did I see such activity, this is what some people had come to believe about that particular organization.

When I accepted my call to preach, this was an issue that I had to deal with. What would be more beneficial, my explaining the tenets of an organization for which I was not recruiting or soliciting new members, or my teaching people about the one true God? Of course the latter is more important than the former and the latter is what I choose. This is because I understand that the time I would waste explaining an organization will do nothing for a person's salvation. Therefore, I had to choose to move away from an organization that I believed in to get people to believe in God. This is because the calling is more important than the organization. Much like the calling should be more important than fame, fortune, or just being different.

Some of us are called to be different. However, being different does not mean changing the word of God. This is what I see many preachers, and pastors doing today. To increase numbers, to grow in size or to grow in fame many of us are doing whatever there is that is possible and claiming to do it in the name of God. Nevertheless, the love for God is not being increased in all of the world and the faith of the people is not being increased as it should be. I am by no means suggesting that women pastors are the reason for the state of things in the church now. However, the movement of women becoming pastors is further evidence of people diminishing or attempting to smother the importance of adhering to the word of God.

It may be true that we should not challenge a person's calling. However, we must try the spirits.

> "Beloved, believe not every spirit, but TRY THE SPIRITS whether they are of God: because many false prophets are gone out into the world" (1 John 4:1).

We learn to try the spirits by what we have from the word of God. As Jesus was tempted in the wilderness by the devil, He tested the devil with what is written in the word of God.

> "And when the tempter came to him, he said, If thou be the Son of God, command that these stones be made bread. But he answered and said, It is written, Man shall not live by bread alone, but by every word that proceedeth out of the mouth of God" (Matthew 4:3-4).

This is also how we must try the Spirit, by what it says in the Word of God. If a woman claims to be called to be pastor or bishop, it is written in 1Timothy that the bishop "must be the husband of one husband of one wife", then where is the permission granted in the Word of God? As Jesus explained to the tempter that, "man shall not live by bread alone," he was reciting the words spoken by God in the book of Deuteronomy. Jesus illustrates to us that the spirits should be tried by the information already recorded in the Word of God.

> "And he humbled thee, and suffered thee to hunger, and fed thee with manna, which thou knewest not, neither did thy fathers know; that he might make thee know that man doth not live by bread only, but by every word that proceedeth out of the MOUTH of the LORD doth man live" (Deuteronomy 8:3)

It is not my suggestion that women who proclaim to be pastors are evil people or even tempters, but we test their position and their calling and their spiritual maturity by the word of God. Of course, this does not just apply to women pastors, but in all cases, we are challenged to draw ourselves to the Word of God to clear up any misrepresentations of the Spirit. In Jesus' temptation, He replied with the word of God. If any spirit or person operates outside of the Word of God, it is a good indication that they do not represent God in what they proclaim to do.

Being pastor is not a calling for anyone able to do the job. God has shown in his word that he can use or get anything to pastor his churches and to accomplish his goals. Yet, He chose men for the position, not birds, not bears, wolves, nor dogs and as indicated in this book, not women

"Pastor," It's Just A Title.

> "And he gave some, **apostles; and** some, **prophets**; and some**, evangelists;** and some**, pastors and teachers**; For the perfecting of the saints, for the work of the ministry, for the edifying of the body of Christ" Till we all come in the unity of the faith, and of the knowledge of the Son of God, unto a perfect man, unto the measure of the stature of the fullness of Christ: That we henceforth be no more children, tossed to and fro, and carried about with every wind of doctrine, by the sleight of men, and cunning craftiness, whereby they lie in wait to deceive; But speaking the truth in love, may grow up into him in all things, which is the head, even Christ: From whom the whole body fitly joined together and compacted by that which every joint supplieth, according to the effectual working in the measure of every part, maketh increase of the body unto the edifying of itself in love" (Ephesians 4:11-16).

I have felt much apprehension around writing this particular book. My apprehension stems from understanding the differing opinions on this subject. It also stems from a sincere desire to avoid offending my fellow brothers and sisters in the ministry. However, as much as I have felt apprehension about writing this book, I know that it was my calling to do so and I hope to bring about some unity in the body of Christ. All of us must understand that God has created all of us for a purpose and that purpose must be accomplished in the position to which we are called. As in the scripture text above, all are not pastors and teachers; all are not evangelists, apostles or prophets. Various positions are there for all of us to occupy.

In the United States, anyone that meets the age criteria and does not have a criminal record can go out and buy a handgun and even a badge yet that will not make them a police officer. They cannot be an officer without the individual taking the pledge of support to the office and the authority of the state, county, city or federal government that can convey some authority. That person would no more be a police officer than the same person who calls themselves a pastor without the proper authority. This authority only comes from God. If one does not like it, then one should not profess to preach the word. Oh, it is understood that someone has to license and ordain each person that preaches and teaches but, as mentioned earlier, the authority to pastor comes from the Lord.

To say that the term Pastor is just a title is just another way of trying to get around what truly is a God given and God appointed position. It is more than just a title; it is more than just a word. It is no different than someone impersonating a police officer, or a doctor, or a lawyer, or a judge, or any other professional position. If a citizen impersonates a police officer and gets caught that citizen will have to pay for what is a known crime.

Just about every citizen, every police officer, every judge knows and understands that there are consequences for such an act as impersonating a professional. Likewise, a general citizen cannot impersonate a doctor without the proper credentials and license because there are certain consequences for committing such an act. As such, no one other than a criminal or someone with an altered sense of reality would consider himself a police officer when they are indeed not a police officer or a lawyer when they are indeed not a lawyer. In fact, no one would call himself or herself a garbage person or a custodian or even an industrial hygienist if they were not. This is because most everyone understands that there is more connected to the title than just it being mere words.

The difference in preachers and pastors is paramount yet very fundamental. All pastors are preachers but not all preachers are pastors. This may be a source of confusion for many. Under normal circumstances, people tend to equate one general position with another more specialized one.

There are many categories for law enforcement personnel and many specialties for doctors. As such, all police officers may be in law enforcement but not all who are in law enforcement are police officers. Some are FBI, some are sheriffs, some are environmental law enforcement and the list goes on. Law enforcement just happens to be the basic discipline for a vast field of individuals. The same is true for doctors and preachers. Not all doctors practice medicine and all preachers do not pastor. Some preachers are called to help, evangelize, or serve the pastor whom they are under.

The confusion caused by the term "pastor" can be easily understood if one is able to, even slightly, understand people. For many, if you mention a term such as doctor, police officer, or preacher, we quickly think of what we normally associate with the term. If our interaction with doctors mostly included those of the medical field, we are probably less likely to think of those in the field of theology, or physics or even education.

The same idea holds true with preachers. Most of us have had our main interaction in the church with seeing, hearing or interacting with the preacher in the church who is most often the pastor. The other terms for preachers are less used and in some cases less known to people in the church so when we hear about the preacher we immediately think of the pastor.

When we look at Ephesians 4:11-16 above, it is easy to see that there are distinct differences between apostle, prophets, evangelist, pastors and teachers. So obviously, there is a distinct difference between the positions that people hold and the titles that they have. It is an important issue because the office of pastor represents the authority that God gave to man.

The reason that it is against the law to impersonate a police officer is because the police officer has the authority of the government that he or she represents. If anyone acts outside of that authority or takes that authority without being duly given it, they do not represent the one who has given the authority but they represent someone who opposes that authority whether it be another government or that individual themselves. Either way the individual is completely out of line and thereby subject to the penalties that come with their violation.

For some reason, it is obvious that people would rather take a title or position that they are clearly unauthorized to take than to operate in the position for which they were truly called. What people know but are reluctant to accept is that God will not call you to a position that makes his word contrary. If He were to do so, He would prove either to be confused or to appear to have changed what He has declared in His word. He has declared in His word that He does not change.

I am amazed that the same people who say that the "word" they preach is the infallible and inerrant word of God still operate as if it is failed or untrue. One thing is clear in all of this and that is that there are three distinct positions on the issue. There is who is right, there is who is wrong, and there is the truth.

I believe that all can agree that the word of God is the truth. I also believe that there are many Christian believers who believe what God says, regardless of how it might strike us or affect us. What that means is that someone is right about what God's position is and someone is wrong. The good thing is that whoever is wrong or incorrect can change their position if they are truly committed to doing and being what God has ordained.

It is clear from the passage in Ephesians 4 that each position is given for the perfecting of the Saints, work of the ministry and edifying of the body of Christ. First, each position is necessary for the equipping of the saints.

The saints need to be thoroughly equipped to be effective in changing the world. The saints are less equipped to enact real change if the church does not have a clear understanding of our individual roles. In addition, the text of Ephesians 4 is especially important in light of the misuse and misinterpretation of Acts 2:17. Acts 2:17 is one of the passages that proponents of women being pastors use to support their position. The passage reads:

> "And it shall come to pass in the last days, saith God, I will pour out of my Spirit upon all flesh: and your sons and your daughters shall prophesy, and your young men shall see visions, and your old men shall dream dreams:" (Acts 2:17).

What these proponents fail to admit or just plain disregard is that the writer is expressing the fulfillment of prophecy within the text itself. One only needs to read verse 16 to know this to be true:

> "But this is that which was spoken by the prophet Joel;" (Acts 2:16).

From this, we can see that Acts 2:17 is misused to support an event that takes place now when it, in fact, has already occurred. I will admit that there is a possibility that this could be a partially fulfilled prophecy that Peter is speaking of, however, in the text, this is not clear. Those who choose to use this scripture do so saying that it proclaims that "daughters" means or includes women being called to be pastors. However, in light of the text in Ephesians 4, it is clear that the ability to prophesy would fall under the gift of a prophet, which is completely different from that of pastor and teacher.

It is possible that one person could work or operate in more than one position at a given time. It is also possible for one person to operate in one and only one position at a given time. As it relates to women being pastor, though they should never operate in or occupy the office of pastor, they could conceivably operate in one or more of the other positions identified. It is clearly more than a title because it is separate from each of the others mentioned and yet it is connected to teaching, which is another one of the qualifications necessary for pastors.

This particular office is much more than a title. What women pastors must understand is that they must vacate their positions as pastor for their own sakes. Not solely because they are women, but more because they have not been given the authority to hold the position. The same as novices having been excluded from being called to the office by the Word of God, women have been excluded by absence of any qualifying conditions.

Some might say that their omission is, in fact, an act of inclusion. This is just not so, once again, the desire to make room for something in the church that is not in the will of God, does not make the act of accommodation correct. Churches do not allow thieves to come in, steal and then say that it is helping the thieves get closer to God. This is just not sane, for when there is nothing left to take at one church, they will seek out another that is just as free giving and never, in reality, will the thief get any closer to God.

If the church allowed sinners to openly sin and accept it as ministry, then the church would be wrong. Ezekiel 3 records these words:

> "When I say unto the wicked, Thou shalt surely die; and thou givest him not warning, nor speakest to warn the wicked from his wicked way, to save his life; the same wicked man shall die in his iniquity; but his blood will I require at thine hand. Yet if thou warn the wicked, and he turn not from his wickedness, nor from his wicked way, he shall die in his iniquity; but thou hast delivered thy soul. Again, When a righteous man doth turn from his righteousness, and commit iniquity, and I lay a stumblingblock before him, he shall die: because thou hast not given him warning, he shall die in his sin, and his righteousness which he hath done shall not be remembered; but his blood will I require at thine hand. Nevertheless if thou warn the righteous man, that the righteous sin not, and he doth not sin, he shall surely live, because he is warned; also thou hast delivered thy soul" (Ezekiel 3:18-21).

The church and its pastors have a responsibility to warn the wicked and the righteous, the saved and the lost, the pastor and the misplaced leader. This is because the Lord wants all of his children to prosper and reach the mark of salvation. The title, Pastor is more than just a title because with it comes great responsibility, great challenge and great reward. This reward will not be received in the world but in the end.

The title cannot be relegated to being just a word that describes someone in clergy or someone that preaches because I hear a number of sermons from unsaved and saved people, people who call themselves pastor and people who call themselves members. However, none of them are authentic without the calling from God, the authority from God and the security in the scriptures.

So even if it were just a title, by virtue of whom it describes and what it represents, it shows that some should not hold the position.

Who Does She Obey?

> "For the husband is the head of the wife, even as Christ is the head of the church and he is the saviour of the body. Therefore as the church is subject unto Christ, so let the wives be to their own HUSBANDS in every thing" (Ephesians 5:23-24).

Who does the woman obey, may be one of the greatest questions posed. The answer provides a not so unique perspective to the subject of leadership. Since the fall of man, as accounted in the book of Genesis, woman was sentenced, by God, to be ruled by her husband;

> "Unto the woman he said, I will greatly multiply thy sorrow and thy conception; in sorrow thou shalt bring forth children; and thy desire shall be to thy husband, and he shall RULE over thee" (Genesis 3:16).

The preceding text was the words of the Almighty God for life after the fall. It can be safely said that the man, prior to the fall, did not rule the woman. This is a safe conclusion because if that were the case then God would have no reason to state or sentence the woman to what he did. This is further understood by the fact that the sentence came after the sin. Prior to Genesis 3:16 one can believe that the two, man and woman were possibly equal in power and authority. Except for the fact that man was created first and their obvious anatomical differences, God had not identified or proclaimed any differences in power or subjection between the man and the woman, prior to the fall.

Presumably, the man and the woman were equally independent and neither was subject to the other. After the fall everything was changed, not by man, but by God. As part of the woman's punishment for her part in the sin, she became subject to the rule of her husband. The word rule here refers to exactly what it implies. The man was to reign or have dominion over the woman from then forward. This was an eternal punishment and not one that was limited just to the life of Eve. This judgment was translated to all women for her sake.

The fact that it was a sentence and that it continues even unto today is clear and evidenced by the first part of the scripture. The Lord said, in Genesis 3:16 above, "I will greatly multiply thy sorrow and thy conception; in sorrow thou shalt bring forth children." For the sake of those who do not understand the King James Version of the Bible I will try to explain what this means in easier to understand terms. What God has decreed upon the woman is pain brought about from conception and pain through child bearing. In other words, the growth of children, in the womb is to be uncomfortable and children would be born out of the pain of the woman.

I have been fortunate enough to be present at the birth of two of my children. Though the atmosphere, the anticipation, the beauty of the entire event was overwhelming, I could see what my wife was dealing with as it relates to pain and her discomfort. I could not feel her pain, Thank God, but I could see the pain on her face and sense the uncomfortable feelings that she was having. I understand that my wife was not unique in this respect. Apparently, most women that give birth endure great pain in the process. I understand that doctors can now hide the pain or trick the body into dismissing the pain, but doctors cannot get rid of the pain all together. Medications treat pain. For medications to be useful there has to be something to treat.

No scripture can be sited that dismisses, nullifies, or otherwise overturns the judgment that God decreed upon woman. As such, women are still to be ruled by their husband as they still endure pain and discomfort in childbirth. Now, for those who get an uncomfortable feeling with the word "rule" as it is used here, there is no need to fret. In light of women's rights, women's liberation and gender equality, it is to say that woman was not sentenced to lead men in relation to biblical, scriptural and evangelical matters. Furthermore, women have not been given power over men in the home. I understand that many women happen to be the breadwinners in the home. However, just like the saying "money can't buy love" it cannot buy a way out of a position that God has placed one in either.

The position God has placed women in is not one of equality to men with respect to leadership in His church but one of inequality to men. This is not to say that they are lesser in importance in any way but they are different. Just as a company only has one CEO at a time, or a country has only one President at a time or one King at a time, so does God's church and a God centered home. Nothing can survive with two rulers or two guides. Two leaders that have opposing views will take the ones they lead, nowhere. This is because if they try to take their followers in different directions, they will either stay where they are or they will split. Either way, progress suffers at the pride, greed or confusion of the leadership.

The preceding challenge is described in the Bible as follows:

> "No man can serve two masters: for either he will hate the one, and love the other; or else he will hold to the one, and despise the other. Ye cannot serve God and mammon" (Matthew 6:24).

Inevitably, a choice will be made for one or the other. The choice made can have far-reaching implications and detrimental results. In the case of the married woman pastor, whom does she love and whom does she hate. I understand that Jesus was not discussing this particular issue, but the concept is the same.

Women that take the position of pastor are put in a precarious position, especially if they are married. Here, there are two things that the Bible makes perfectly clear. First, the pastor takes his direction from God, especially concerning matters within the church. Second, women have been commanded and they are expected to obey their husbands. This inevitably puts her under two "heads" if she is also pastor. The position is precarious because women pastors are forced into a position that they now have to choose whom they will obey. Having to make a choice is not so much a problem as what the choice means. The choice means certain sin, brought about by God, in effect making the Word of God a lie.

God often directs his leaders, through His Holy Spirit, to do certain things, i.e. build, go to a church, visit a place, give something, or hold back from something. These are not unusual occurrences for pastors, prophets, children of God, ministers or leaders. Consider the following scenario: God tells the woman pastor of the church that she will need to go to another state to minister, or visit a rough area of town or deal with an unforeseen issue that will take her to unknown, unexplored places. In the same scenario, say that her husband disagrees with what she says God has told her to do and tells her not to do it. She would be right as pastor to do what God has told her to do, but she commits a sin against the Word of God if she disobeys her husband. She would also be right if she obeyed her husband but she would then be wrong because she disobeyed God. Would God force any of his leaders into a position that there was no way out but to sin? Of course not, God would not make His children sin neither would He break any of his promises. Most of all, His word cannot be made into a lie.

All people of faith, especially pastors, have a responsibility to obey God at all times, especially when there are issues regarding the faith and ministry. This does not imply that all people or all pastors maintain this responsibility but it is what is required. If the pastor must answer to someone in addition to God, then there is a conflict presented for that person. Married women have to answer to their husbands as required by the word of God. As it is written in Hebrews 13:17: "Obey them that have the rule over you, and submit yourselves: for they watch for your souls, as they that must give account, that they may do it with joy, and not with grief: for that is unprofitable for you."

It is understandable that some women might say they do not fall under this rule because they are not married. However, before they get too far ahead of themselves and think that they are not bound, the Word of God addresses all women as follows:

> "But I would have you know, that the HEAD of every man is Christ; and the HEAD of the woman is the man; and the HEAD of Christ is God" (1 Corinthians 11:3).

There is no mistaking the headship that has been authorized and ordained by Almighty God. In this scripture, there is a clear distinction of order between man and woman. This is especially important for those who would like to contend that the Bible refers to all of mankind when it speaks of "man." While this may be true in some scriptural text, it is unmistakable that it refers to man as a gender in others. But in 1 Corinthians 11:3 the separation is made clear and when it says "man", it is understood to mean all men and when it says "woman", it means all women. In case one might not believe it to mean all, the word "every" is added before man to show that God means all.

This gives us all the complete illustration of the order of relationship between man and woman, and man and God. While some would have us to believe that there is either no order or that there is some modified order with God, this is not true. Some would have us to believe, in the absence of scriptural support, that men and women stand equal before God. While we may be equal in regards to salvation, reward, gifts, etc., there is an obvious difference illustrated here. While we know from faith that God and Christ are one and equal, there is an obvious difference illustrated. Jesus reduced himself to serve as mediator between God and us.

> "Let this mind be in you, which was also in Christ Jesus: Who, being in the form of God, **thought it not robbery to be equal with God**: But made himself of no reputation, and **took** upon him the form of a servant, and was made in the likeness of men: And being found in fashion as a man, he humbled himself, and became obedient unto death, even the death of the cross" (Philippians 2:5-8).

While Jesus is clearly God and equal to God, he did not think it necessary to hold on to the position but rather give it up to save us. For that reason, instead of us remaining disconnected from God as in the illustration below, Jesus reconnected us to God as we were created to be.

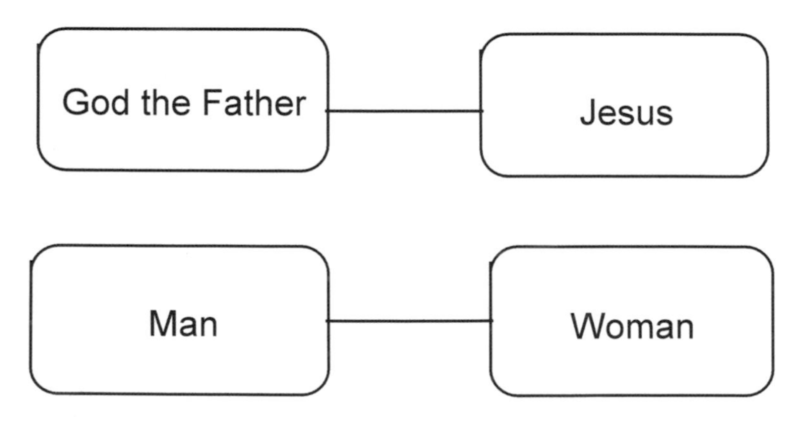

With the above illustration, there was no connection to God for man prior to Jesus Christ reducing himself. It should be understood that there was a pseudo connection through the earlier priesthood, but mankind overall was disconnected. We are fortunate that Jesus lowered himself and in doing so he, from what the Bible says in 1 Corinthians 11:3, returned us to connection with the Father. We can visualize it with the following illustration:

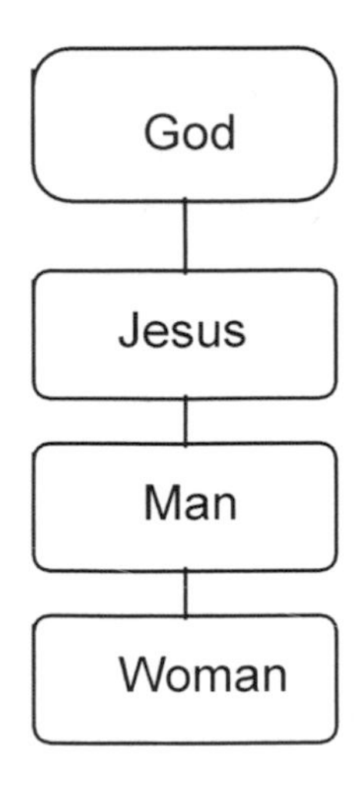

So if God proclaimed men as the head of women, why is there a debate? From the scriptures, we can see the order between God, Christ, man, and woman. No part of the body can do anything without the head, whether it be naturally speaking or supernaturally speaking. If there is someone that does not believe in the headship that God has established then they do not believe the whole Word of God and therefore cannot be trusted to preach or teach the gospel. Clearly, I am not saying that all women pastors fail to regard the Word of God with reverence and hold it to be as powerful as it is; however, women pastors would have to find it difficult to preach the Word while being so out of line with the Word.

Consider the following scripture:

> "For the body is not one member, but many. If the foot shall say, Because I am not the hand, I am not of the body; is it therefore not of the body? And if the ear shall say, Because I am not the eye, I am not of the body; is it therefore not of the body? If the whole body were an eye, where were the hearing? If the whole were hearing, where were the smelling? But now hath God set the members every one of them in the body, as it hath pleased him. And if they were all one member, where were the body? But now are they many members, yet but one body. And the eye cannot say unto the hand, I have no need of thee: nor again the head to the feet, I have no need of you. Nay, much more those members of the body, which seem to be more feeble, are necessary:" (1 Corinthians 12:14-22).

From the text above, it is clear that the head cannot be the foot or the hand. The head cannot be the legs or the arms either. No part of the body can come before or control the head and the head is always in control over all of the body. Nowhere does the Bible declare that the woman is to be over the man in any regard, especially in the church. Moreover, if she has not received authority over those under her, how then can she lead them? She cannot because then she would be out of order. Furthermore, how does one come to rule over another that has been given rule over them? Parents must train their children; children are not expected to train their parents. The world tends to look poorly at parents that do not train their children "adequately". Husbands have received God's authorization to rule their wives; wives have not received such authorization.

If man is at the head of woman, woman cannot be at the head of man also. Pastors, by definition, or position, are the directors or "heads" of the church until Jesus returns for his church.

Pastors are the head of the church as the leader of the church and no "body" is good with two heads because it is torn if the heads try to go in different directions. As such, there is no such position as "co-pastor" that would suffice for the operation of the church either. Many wives stand as co-pastors with their husbands over some churches. However this is problematic as well because it means that should something happen to the pastor, the wife becomes pastor. This is still not supported by the Word of God.

Many women struggle with being told that their husbands have rule over them. Many women, in light of the worldview concerning equality, ability, and women's rights, tend to take issue with or have a problem with being told to submit or even be obedient to their husbands. However, the Word of God records the following:

> "The aged women likewise, that they be in behaviour as becometh holiness, not false accusers, not given to much wine, teachers of good things; That they may teach the young women to be sober, to love their husbands, to love their children, To be discreet, chaste, keepers at home, good, **obedient** to their own husbands, that the word of God be not blasphemed" (Titus 2:3-5)

From this it is easy to see that wives being "obedient" to their husbands is not some cult view that came about to keep women oppressed. This is the view given in the Word of God from the beginning of life, after the fall of man in the Garden of Eden. Obedience is further reminded to be taught to young women as a practice to maintain the integrity of the Word of God.

The issue is not whether women are capable of being pastor, it is whether they have been given the authority to be, hold, or occupy the office of pastor. The scriptures instruct all of us to obey the Word of God and keep his commandments. It does not eliminate any part of the Word of God. In fact obeying His word is an act of love shown towards God. In essence, anyone that eliminates, omits, or disregards any of the Word of God does not show love towards him. Everyone should know, especially those of the faith, that all authority is given by God. Whether to kings, queens, presidents, or pastors, all authority is given and ordained by God.

God has encouraged or commanded women to obey their husbands and he has decreed that woman is ruled by her husband so how then can a woman be placed in a position of leadership or headship over her husband or over the man? She cannot because, once again, she would be out of order.

From the scripture in Ephesians 5:23-24 there is a certain beauty to the descriptive way Paul conveys his message. Two things are evident in the text. First, the husband is comparable to Christ and the wife is comparable to the church. Both have separate and distinct roles that are further outlined in Ephesians 5, but the above text is especially powerful. Paul says that wives should be subject to their husband in every thing. Generally, nothing is left out of "every thing" and all things would be included in "every thing." Therefore, it would include even issues on church matters for the married woman pastor. This could possibly hinder the direction for a church pastored by a woman, if they believe and obey the word.

There is a reason for this unhindered leadership in the church. Throughout the Bible, the men that God used were chosen because they were not subject to anyone but God. If God gave an order then the men followed it even if they were not Kings or leaders, God's chosen men knew that they should only obey God. This is not possible for women, whether married or not they would still have some subjection or subordination to men according to 1 Corinthians 11:3.

If the Bible declares that men are the head of women then that means that women would never be the head of men unless God's Word is a lie or His Word has changed. Some may say that the scripture provides for these out of order conditions. If that is indeed the case, then the same people must believe that men can be above Christ in the same hierarchy. If this is the belief of these individuals, then they should not be followed at any time whether male or female.

The love of God must abound at all times in all matters of faith. As such, women should not deplore their God ordained and God given position but embrace it.

Queen Esther understood her position as a subject to her husband. In saving the lives of her people, she did the most from the position that God had ordained for her to be in at the time. She did not consider doing anything from any other position than that of Queen. In addition, even knowing the potential consequences, she did not use any deception or tricks to accomplish her goal. All women can be powerful women of God if they chose to serve God from the position he has decreed and ordained for them.

If we say that she can pastor, then who is the head of the home? If she pastors and cannot be the head of the home, who then does she obey? This is an issue that cannot be left untouched because if she can lead one of these, is she also the one that God puts in charge of the other? I was reared in a single parent household, so I understand the capabilities that a woman has to persevere and to overcome many obstacles but how does one justify or even attempt to overcome the Word of God?

Clear Word, Clear Choice, Pastors Must Be Men

> "This is a true saying, If a man desire the office of a bishop, he desireth a good work. A bishop then must be blameless, the husband of one wife, vigilant, sober, of good behaviour, given to hospitality, apt to teach; A bishop then must be blameless, the husband of one wife, vigilant, sober, of good behaviour, given to hospitality, apt to teach; Not given to wine, no striker, not greedy of filthy lucre; but patient, not a brawler, not covetous; One that ruleth well his own house, having his children in subjection with all gravity; (For if a man know not how to rule his own house, how shall he take care of the church of God?) Not a novice, lest being lifted up with pride he fall into the condemnation of the devil. Moreover he must have a good report of them which are without; lest he fall into reproach and the snare of the devil" (1 Timothy 3:1-7).

God has clearly illustrated in his word that women are not to hold the office of the Pastor. Love it or hate it, the word is clear. Various scriptures provide guidance to the church as to the structure of the chosen, anointed and appointed leadership. Much like David was anointed to be King, the pastor is anointed to be pastor. The anointing, just like in David's case, comes from

God first and not man. Although it was a man that anointed David with oil to ordain Him as God's chosen King, it was God that directed Samuel in who to seek out and anoint. With this, it is easier to see how some women may feel that man does not have a say because many of them may truly believe that God has anointed them for the position. Now, that would be the end of the debate if it were not for the Word of God that does not support that being the end of the issue.

What we believe, except in the case of miracles, must line up line up with scripture. This is not to say that miracles are not to be believed. Miracles, of course do not fit this understanding because miracles defy what we know to be logical. Selection for the office of pastor occurred before we were born and thereby are not miracles, in the supernatural sense. We know this to be true from what God told the prophet in the book of Jeremiah: "Before I formed thee in the belly I knew thee; and before thou camest forth out of the womb I sanctified thee, and I ordained thee a prophet unto the nations" (Jeremiah 1:5). Clearly, God knows all of his creation before they are.

The scriptures that clearly identify God's will for his chosen church leader are provided to us in what are more commonly referred to as the Pastoral Epistles. It is a wonder, to me, how so many people are able to disregard this unambiguous, and purposely placed proof of who may and who may not be the pastor or bishop of the church.

Many people may even try to go as far as saying that the term used in the Bible "bishop" is completely separate and different from the term pastor. While it may be true that the terms by definition are different, it is even truer that the terms and their representation are 100 percent identical. When Paul speaks of the leader of the church and calls them "bishop," it is known that he is indeed speaking of the leader of an individual church as well as the leader of a collection of churches. Either way Paul's position is clear. When we look at the text that Paul writes to his young student Timothy, it is clear to see what Paul's position is as it deals with the leader of the local church. Furthermore, it is a clear understanding by most in the church realizing that the letters to Timothy are regularly considered a part of the "pastoral epistles".

Some may try to advocate that Paul was sexist or against women altogether. This is untrue, through his many references to the women that supported him and the ministry, Paul showed great gratitude. In many instances, Paul saluted the women in his letters for their work in the ministry. This makes it difficult to believe that Paul was totally against women. Even if that were true, one cannot contend with the written word of God. If the passages in the Bible can be discounted in any way, then our faith is made worthless. Paul apparently understood that some people still doubted his words at times and wrote the following words for our assurance:

> "If any man thinks himself to be a prophet or spiritual, let him acknowledge that the things which I write to you are the commandments of the Lord" (1 Corinthians 14:37).

These are very powerful words when you delve into what he is really saying. Clearly, he is challenging those of the faith to accept what he says as coming from the Lord. This should not be at all difficult for the members of the body who claim to "preach the word." One cannot pick and choose what part of the 'Word" to use, one must preach all of the "Word." If we are indeed spiritual as mentioned in the scripture above, then we must believe what Paul writes as commandments or directions from God. That is, we cannot discount Paul's words because they are indeed the words of the Lord. We also cannot discount the words of Paul because they do not help our particular position. This saying would hold true for all of the scriptures for which Paul is recognized as the author.

For those who would say that readers could discount or omit a portion of what Paul has written, they must also agree that we should omit all of what he has written. The Bible is, once again, the complete, infallible Word of God. Furthermore, those people who would like to omit parts would be better served if the books written and attributed to Paul did not exist. However, what would become of the fruit of the spirit Paul wrote in his letter to the Galatians? What would become of the Christian's inheritance that he wrote about in his letter to the Ephesians? What would we be if we did not have what he told us about our ability to do anything through the power of Christ in his letter to the Philippians? The list can go on and on describing the foundation that Paul has provided for the Christian faith.

It is difficult to see how eliminating more than 50% of the New Testament would help the Christian faith. This is because if people were or are allowed to eliminate Paul's writings from the Bible then they would eliminate fourteen complete books of the New Testament. This would not be an issue save for the Lord telling his people to not add to nor take away from his word. Paul's contribution to the faith and the church has provided the foundation for the church today. What will people do if movements that go against the Word of God are allowed to prevail without any correction or declaration against them? Apparently churches would have to make up the rules as they saw fit to do and the chaos that is, questionably, not so detrimental to the people of God now, may indeed become detrimental.

God's clarity as to who should or should not be a pastor/ bishop does not come from Paul's letter the Romans, nor does it come from either of his letters to the Corinthians or even the letter to the church at Galatia. No, it was written to his young ministers Timothy and Titus. He first writes it to Timothy and later to Titus in different but similar words. Paul salutes the young minister early in the letter to acknowledge himself as the author of the letter. Many scholars debate who authored which books in the Bible. However, this is not the case for the letters written to Timothy and Titus. Since there is no need to verify their authorship, we can explore their purpose.

Clearly, the letters to Timothy were written to Timothy and clearly, they were written to address the organizing of the church, the selection of the necessary leadership and the preaching of the gospel. Paul, in speaking to Timothy, also spoke to all ministers to pray, to believe and to teach.

The scriptures 1 Timothy 3 and Titus 1:6-7 both give us the definitive answer to the question of who should be or could be pastor. There is no play on words necessary, no interpretation is needed to enhance the real understanding of what the scripture says and means in this case. In fact, people who avoid using the scripture to justify their position do so as a means to deceive. Others just may not know what the scriptures say concerning the issue.

When one looks at the biblical qualifications for bishops/pastors/head of the church, the deciding words come from the qualifications themselves. In his letter to Timothy, Paul begins this discussion with these words "This is a true saying, If a man desires the office of a bishop …" How pastors, men and women, get around this is unknown. It is not understood if people skip the word "man" or treat it as the universal understanding of "mankind" in this instance, yet it clearly is talking about the male gender here.

Another key to point out from this particular text is the writer's opening. He does not open with some arbitrary or ambiguous salute. He begins by acknowledging that the words are true. Truth is what all Christians should strive to obtain. Truth is what we have been given as our key to salvation. Here we are told bluntly that the saying is true.

As one reads the text, one can see that the writer never uses the terms she or her in the descriptive attributes for the bishop. Even if it were possible to take out the "he" and "his" in the qualifications (see 1st Timothy 3) and replace them with "she's" or "her" or "they", one would still not be able to change or discount the definitiveness of the second verse in the chapter.

As discussed previously, Paul explained in 1 Corinthians 14:37 that if anyone thinks himself a prophet or spiritual, let them acknowledge that the words that he (Paul) writes, are the commandments of God. Commandments require the one being commanded to obey the words of the one giving the command. Keeping commandments are one of the core responsibilities for all people, especially Christians. In looking at the biblical qualifications for pastors/bishops one can see that they are indeed numerous and achievable. However, one of the qualifications makes no mistake about who can be the leader of the church.

The second verse of 1 Timothy Chapter 3 says that the man who desires the office of a bishop must be "the husband of one wife." These five words make no mistake about who should or should not be the leader of the church. This qualification in itself disqualifies all women from holding or sitting in the official seat of a bishop, pastor or even a deacon when you read further. These words are definitive because it is understood that from the beginning, the man was known as the husband and the woman has was known as his wife. In the book of Genesis, after God had created the woman for Adam, this is what is written:

> "And they were both naked, the man and his wife, and were not ashamed" (Genesis 2:25).

These words were written after the forming of the woman. As she was created, the woman was the man's wife. This is important to understand because some may try to mislead people by saying that the husband of one wife could mean or be translated spouse of one spouse, woman of one man, or some other perversion of the scriptures. This is not possible in this text because throughout the Bible, these two words always mean the same thing. The husband is the male figure in the marriage relationship and the wife is the female figure in the marriage relationship. Armed with this infallible understanding, it is thoroughly clear, through scripture, that women were not authorized to hold the office of pastor.

Here, there is no ambiguity, no loose ends, and no hidden mystery in the scripture and therefore no room for debate. Yet many will argue the point as if God has somehow changed his mind from what He inspired Paul to write to Timothy. As difficult as it may be to accept the Word of God as truth in this age, it cannot be made a lie to suit our or your own individual purposes and desires.

In the book of 1st Peter we find that God ascribes to Jesus, the title of bishop.

> "For ye were as sheep going astray; but are now returned unto the Shepherd and Bishop of your soul" (1st Peter 2:25).

This text should impart to all the importance of the office of bishop. This scripture should illustrate that the word is not merely a generic term to describe a simplistic office to be held by just any one. This text should illustrate that the office is one of high regard and one that has been assigned to the individuals for which it was designed. From this, it can be seen that the title of bishop is important enough for God to ascribe it to Jesus. The pastor of the church is considered the shepherd of the flock and he must protect and lead it to Jesus with all diligence. Obviously, this position is not one to be played with or abused by children of the true and living God if it is also one shared by the only birthed Son of God.

The grace of God has brought salvation to every person. However, grace is more pronounced, or more evident in the absence of obedience. That is, the more people sin, the more grace is given: "Moreover the law entered, that the offence might abound. But where sin abounded, grace did much more abound: That as sin hath reigned unto death, even so might grace reign through righteousness unto eternal life by Jesus Christ our Lord" (Roman 5:20-21).

This is why all of us have to do our very best to operate in the calling to which we have been called that we might not confuse or take away from the word of God in any way.

Rather Sacrifice Than Obey.

Obeying the Word of God should come above everything that we as preachers, pastors, and ministers would like to do. I would like all who read this book to know that those of us called to be ministers, preachers and called to do the will of God are also people who have to deal with the issues that face us everyday much the same as unbelievers and others who are not called into the ministry. Though our paths may be different, our journeys are quite the same. Some are stronger at resisting temptation than others. Some find it easier to eliminate vices than others do. Some are more obedient than others are. The issues are centered more in the individual than in their calling. Of course, I do not profess to be the spokesperson for such a large and anointed group of believers. However, the point is made as a reference for understanding that even God's anointed and appointed ministers and preachers can and sometimes do make mistakes.

Moses, a messenger of God, was punished for his disobedience to God. The children of Israel were punished as a group under the leadership of Joshua because of one person's disobedience to the words and will of God. Disobedience to the words of God caused Samuel to declare to Saul:

> "And Samuel said, Hath the LORD as great delight in burnt offerings and sacrifices, as in obeying the voice of the LORD?

Behold, to obey is better than sacrifice, and to hearken than the fat of rams" (1 Samuel 15:22).

Of course, it would be easier to do what we wanted to do in hope of pleasing God. But this is what led Samuel to deliver the above words. Saul, in an effort to appease and please the people, allowed himself to turn from the words of the Lord and turn from what God had said to him. He disobeyed the Words of the Lord and he was stripped of his office as king. Is it possible that many of the women who call themselves pastor could be working to please and appease others? If so, then they are out of order in the church.

I understand the frustration that some women may feel especially when they feel that they are being held back from doing something that is felt deep within. What our sisters in Christ must do is pray and seek God for an answer to their rightful position in the body. The Bible clearly indicates that their rightful position is not at the head, but that does not mean that it is not on the shoulder, the hand, or even the eye. For where would the body be if the hand did not provide protection for the head at times? More than that, where would the body go if the eye did not show it the way?

To know what the Bible says and continue on the path that does not line up with the word of God is disobedient to God. Women may prove that they are just as capable as men in pastoring but they prove their point in disobedience. One sin does not equal or make another less of a sin.

Obedience is important not just because there are consequences to disobedience, obedience is important because God loves obedience. God rewards obedience and God prefers obedience. Are we as people so different? Wouldn't we all rather that others just did what was asked of them and not question or push back? This is what most people would prefer in their lives.

Things seem to flow much more smoothly when others do what we ask. We often find it easier to deal with our own missteps if people did what we asked. Because God cannot and will not fail, we should be able to understand that there is a purpose behind His design. It may not be revealed to us now or it may have already been revealed and we have missed it but in everything He does, there is a purpose and a reason.

Being disobedient will not weaken or reduce the effectiveness of His Word but it will not be strengthen in the life of the believer either. God's Word gains strength in the minds and hearts of believers when they see it work as it is supposed to and when they see it work in the lives of obedient people. When the prophets of God failed to obey God's Word, the people suffered. The same happens today with such issues as women as pastor, and gay preachers or adulterous leaders.

If we go against what the Bible says, or if we try to finagle different meanings to the Word of God to suit our own purposes, then the people are hurt because they lack the knowledge necessary to trust God completely. People began to trust man and not God when man can turn the Word of God into a lie and cause people to believe that God embraces the missteps of His children. Our task as children of God is to "hate the sin but love the sinner." To do this, we must provide loving correction when necessary and when possible.

It is truly necessary to offer this book because, as was the case with Saul, the called of God will suffer a greater punishment than the children that they touch, influence or lead. Saul's sacrifice literally was the ox and sheep that he allowed to be spared in disobedience to God's Word. Saul's sacrifice ultimately was the loss of his position as king as God had appointed and anointed him.

There Is A Consequence.

Most people understand that there are consequences for doing anything. Whether the consequence is reward or punishment depends on the positions of the judge and the recipient. As an example, look at the task of training a favorite pet. When we are training our pets, especially our dogs, some experts say that it is good to offer them a treat for doing what you asked them to do and keep the treat away from them if they do not do what you would like. When this is done, the pet tends to associate the reward with the completion of the task. With this, the trainer and the pet get something that they desire. However, the reward becomes expected and the pet may falloff if the reward falls off. Similarly, people oftentimes correlate that when God has not punished them for something that they should have received punishment for as a blessing.

It seems that we, as people, get confused because God blesses us even when we are doing wrong. People tend to act as if God does not bless us if we do wrong. To be clear, God does not bless his children for doing wrong, but he does bless us even if we do or have done wrong. This is primarily due to a misunderstanding of what God's blessings are. Our society is more wrapped up in believing God for the "big" blessings that He performs in our lives. We all would be well served to acknowledge that He blesses us every day with air to breathe, life to live, and an opportunity to please Him. The car to drive, home to live in, and jobs that we are able to maintain, are all blessings but there are many, many more blessings we receive and would see if we just took the time to acknowledge them.

Just because He blesses us does not mean that we are in His will or even living the way He has asked us to live. In fact, the Bible declares in Matthew 5:44-45:

> "But I say unto you, Love your enemies, bless them that curse you, do good to them that hate you, and pray for them which despitefully use you, and persecute you; That ye may be the children of your Father which is in heaven: for he maketh his sun to rise on the evil and on the good, and sendeth rain on the just and on the unjust" (Matthew 5:44-45).

The above scripture clearly indicates that God does for good people and bad people. We must do more as His children than the person that does not know Him. One of the things that we can do is keep His commandments and follow the rules and mandates that He has established because if we do not then we too can fall to the same fate as an unbeliever.

Paul, the author of more than 50% of the New Testament, is considered an apostle as a result of his personal experience with Jesus. He has clearly indicated his passion for the ministry, his love for God and his authority for establishing churches in his writings. Paul lets us all know that even the most passionate of us in ministry can end up left out if we do not carefully control ourselves.

> "And every man that striveth for the mastery is temperate in all things. Now they do it to obtain a corruptible crown; but we an incorruptible. I therefore so run, not

> as uncertainly; so fight I, not as one that beateth the air: But I keep under my body, and bring it into subjection: lest that by any means, when I have preached to others, I myself should be a castaway" (1 Corinthians 9:25-27).

Paul is talking about himself as preaching to many people and if he does not control himself, he could end up as a castaway. This, of course, is after he has believed, this is after he has accepted Jesus Christ as his Lord and he still explains that if he does not maintain, he could be lost. This is important because it draws into account the understanding that we, who are of the faith, must be vigilant in our task to reach others, but careful to not lose ourselves.

Paul makes it perfectly clear that his pursuit of others, to lead to salvation should not cost him his own salvation if by virtue of his activities he should fail to control himself and his actions. This would also remain true for those who would contend that they are not wrong because they are saving many people and doing the will of God.

Many people tend to get wrapped up in the consequences that may be a part of or felt during this life but I believe that the consequence can be much greater. The following words are recorded in the Gospel of Matthew:

> "Not every one that saith unto me, Lord, Lord, shall enter into the kingdom of heaven; but he that doeth the will of my Father which is in heaven. Many will say to me in that day, Lord, Lord, have we not prophesied in thy name? and in thy name have cast out devils? and in thy name done many wonderful works? And then will I profess unto them, I never knew you: depart from me, ye that work iniquity" (Matthew 7:21-23).

In this same chapter Jesus Christ discusses false prophets that come in sheep's clothing yet on the inside they are ravenous wolves. Some scholars claim, that in the above text, that Jesus does not say that the individuals who will make these proclamations completed these many works. By the same token, Jesus does not say that they did not accomplish these works either. Indeed, Jesus speaks as though the people that make these claims actually did what they said. The inference is more on the way they did these things and that their methods were some of the iniquity that they worked.

Who are some individuals that could fall into the condemnation of which Jesus speaks? Pastors and ministers are subject to such a fate if the word of God is not clearly and reverently preached. False prophets could fall into such a serious fate as well. Those who have misused the gifts of the spirit for personal gain and fame are subject to such a fate. In addition, those who would misuse the office of pastor or even occupy the office and not have been called to the office would be subject to such a fate if their choice was to continue and act as if the truth had not been revealed to them.

Jesus proclaims that he will say He "never knew you." This is understandable because he only knows those whom God has called. His sheep hear His voice and follow him and he says that He knows us because we have heard his voice. His voice speaks clearly through His word.

As troubling as it may be to hear that Jesus would turn some away in the day of judgment, Christians and others must understand what He truly is saying. Essentially, it can be concluded that He is speaking of something that Paul similarly speaks of in 1 Corinthians 9. The people that Jesus speaks to are obviously believers because they say that they accomplished all of these things in the name of Jesus. Note that they ask Jesus to acknowledge that they prophesied, cast out devils, and did many "wonderful" works in His name.

Now, these people that Jesus is speaking to have apparently been doing the work that is associated with kingdom building. For those who would assert that these people were not saved and were not true believers, I would draw their attention to the act of casting out devils. Jesus was accused of casting out devils by the power of satan in Matthew 12:24-31. In this particular passage, Jesus explains that a Kingdom divided against itself, in essence cannot stand or grow. It is ludicrous to think that a Kingdom that desires to grow would stifle its own growth by increasing then reducing itself as in the case of casting out devils. The devil or any being on his side would not benefit from reducing their own ranks.

The people that Jesus speaks of in Matthew 7 would not proclaim to have cast out devils in the name of Jesus if they did not believe in Jesus and the same holds true for the other miracles that these individuals proclaim. They are dismissed for some reason from the presence of Christ and nothing further is given for their ultimate fates. However, when you read more of the judgment of the nations in Matthew 25 you can see that at the separation, some will be sent away for not having helped others. This is quite possibly the same fate for those that Jesus sends away in Matthew 7 and can be a possible consequence for pastors that do not do what God has said. This is also a possible consequence for those who have built great ministries of size but operate outside of the word of God. Women, that act as or serve as pastor, operate outside of the word of God. As such, they, quite possibly, could also be included in the condemnation that Jesus discussed.

That is not the only proof of there being a consequence when we depart from the faith. In his instructions to Timothy, Paul wrote:

> "Take heed unto thyself, and unto the doctrine; continue in them: for in doing this thou shalt both save thyself, and them that hear thee" (1 Timothy 4:16).

This is further proof that the ministers of the gospel have a responsibility to take heed unto their own words and their own teaching. Remembering that the pastor is the leader and director of the church, Paul gives Timothy and all that follow, this warning to adhere to the faith because if they do this, they will save themselves and others that they preach and teach to. The alternative is failing to hold to the doctrine in which the consequence would be that Timothy would not save himself or them that hear him. In essence, unless there is some obscure scripture in the Bible that explicitly includes women as authorized to be church pastor or bishop, women who have placed themselves in the position or been placed in the position, by men, must step aside. They must step aside to preserve the integrity of the word and they must step aside to keep from losing their own salvation.

God is one hundred percent clear in His desire for all men to be saved and that none should perish, even those who would claim to be saving others as a cavalier stance against gender injustice. God is a just God and if He desired for women to pastor, He would not have been so clear in His word as to the qualifications for His pastor. One must meet the qualifications the same as you would qualify for anything else. If one fails to meet any of the qualifications, one is literally disqualified from the position or opportunity they desire. If one takes something that one has been disqualified from, then that person is a violator of the rules that they say they uphold and stand on. Furthermore, even though they may take the position, the judging authority maintains the right to uphold the disqualification and whatever accomplishments made by the disqualified do not change the state of the disqualified. The qualifications in this case are the Words of God.

There Is No Change In God.

There are some people, some who are members or leaders of large congregations, which would have the church believe that God has changed in some way from what he has always been. Some would have the church believe that the God of Abraham, Isaac, and Jacob is no longer a God of judgment, wrath, and vengeance. They would have the church believe that the just God that destroyed Sodom and Gomorrah for their sins does not look at sin the same way. They would have the church believe that the jealous God who declared that there should be no other God before Him is no longer the same jealous God. The premise behind this belief is that the God of the New Testament is vastly different from the God of the Old Testament.

People want to pursue this route of understanding as a way to interject that God's Word does not fully convey God's will. If He has changed then the words recorded in the Bible may be complete and infallible as it relates to the past. However, they would have us believe that the word is not as complete for the present or the future issues. They would have us believe that the incompleteness, that they attempt to exploit, makes allowances for new things in the church. They may not say this bluntly, but the message becomes clear when what they do attempts to erase or in some way nullify what is written in the scriptures.

This view is flawed in light of God's word spoken in the book of Malachi:

> "For I am the LORD, **I change not**; therefore ye sons of Jacob are not consumed" (Malachi 3:6).

God, by sheer virtue of His nature, does not have to change. This is heavily influenced by the fact that He has the ability to cause everything around Him to change. He can speak a change in men and they would change. He speaks life and things grow. He speaks peace and the winds and waves obey. So for people to think that such a God that is capable of such great miracles and wonders needs to change Himself or His methods is insulting, to say the least. It is insulting to think that a God who can change anything is small enough to make man so important that instead of changing His creation He would change himself.

God loves mankind indeed, but He loves man enough to hold man accountable to the rules that He has created for man. Would that love be any different from a mother's love? Would a mother with a disobedient child show her great love for her child by relaxing the rules to get her child to get in line? It is important to understand that God does not have to bring Himself down to man's level to be effective. What He does is a mystery even unto the greatest of us and we must grow toward Him for us to be effective.

Those that would suggest that God is different or God is doing a new thing misrepresent God and mislead the children of God. It is possible that God may be doing a new thing in different people's lives, but this does not correlate to God changing His person or His purpose to make life easier for mankind.

Of course, the position of expressing that God has changed works for those who would pervert the word of God for personal reasons. That is, one can be much more justified if one accepts the word of God in essence but defy the Word of God in practice. It appears that the various movements taking place in the world today are being allowed to infiltrate the church. Church leaders are failing to stand up for the word of God under the pretense of showing that the church can be just as inclusive as the world. Does anyone else see this as a problem when the church is supposed to be the influence in the world?

It is amazing to see how much of the world system has migrated into the church and how little of the church has filtrated into the world. I, like you, see larger churches, larger congregations, and larger groups of "religious" people. However, in those groups we are challenged to find true lovers of God. Of these larger, bigger, and better-looking churches, we see fewer people that have changed. This is problematic especially for those in ministry that would reduce the creator and exalt the created. The latter has been accomplished, in part, by people claiming that God has changed and that He is somehow different from what we have read.

By reducing the influence of God in the church, the church has essentially eliminated the fear of God from the psyche of the people of God. For some reason, we have succumbed to the people's desire to hear less about what the consequences of sin are and interjected the people's desire to hear what makes them prosperous, what makes them feel good, what makes them feel superior and what makes them feel like Christians. Unfortunately, Christianity is none of these things. In the thrill of building bigger and larger churches, the people are remaining lost. Even though our church buildings are full, the people that fill them are empty. Emptied of the one thing that they would go to church for and that is the assurance of a real connection to the Almighty God.

God does not change but He knew that men would. If men and God changed, what would be the constant in our faith? In any religion, the only constant is the god that the people serve.

However if God is the one that has changed, why would He tell the believer to change, even in their relationship to the world?

God gives us the following words to be help the believer be mindful of our own predisposition to be like others:

> "And be not conformed to this world: but be ye transformed by the renewing of your mind, that ye may prove what is that good, and acceptable, and perfect, will of God" (Romans 12:2).

These are compelling words written to the church. In them, we are told first to not conform to the world that we live in. The message here is straightforward. There is very little interpretation needed to understand this mandate. Clearly, the believer must avoid doing what everyone else does or in some cases what may appear to work for everyone else. The believer is told, in the above passage, to not be like the world and not try to look like the world or even imitate the world.

This appears to be difficult for our present day churches to do since many of them have replaced the pulpit with a stage for performances. Some of these performances are touted as praise and worship services when, in essence, most of them are nothing more than personal jam sessions for some musicians, singers and dancers. I believe that there is a place in worship and praise for some singing and some dancing. I even believe that there is room for "radical praise" in our services. What I do not believe is that the church must become the modern day club scene to reach people who want to make a change for God. For when the music, dancing or songs change, these people tend to change as well. They change churches. This tends to happen because the methods that were used to draw them was not the Word of God. It was the more a result of the groups, the activities, the concerts, or the food. Cut out the activities, and oftentimes, you cut out the people because they had received very little God.

It is also written in the scripture, that the believer should be transformed by renewing their minds. The beauty in this passage is the fact that God gives the believer the answer to how they would transform themselves. It is not by continuing along a dead end path. It is not by changing the music that you might listen too. It is not even by moving and trying to change your physical environment. The key to changing oneself is to completely and personally renew your mind. What this means simply is to rejuvenate your mind, to refresh it with new ideas, good ideas, godly ideas, it is what most adolescents do when they decide to stop traveling a path of destruction to start traveling a path not so cluttered with the consequences of bad decisions.

It is a change that most believers have had to make as a result of coming into a realization of the presence of God in their life. It is a change that must be maintained by periodically renewing the mind to eliminate troublesome issues that come into our lives to challenge us and to test our resolve. It is a change that can only be made by the individual, a family member cannot make it, nor can a friend make it. The ability, and the necessity for mankind to change, does not equate or even allude to God having to make similar changes.

Can God change? The short answer is yes. The question is not as to his ability to change. God, of course, is able to do anything. The question is more a matter as to why would men rather God change? Understanding the answer to this particular question makes it easier to understand why issues that God does not like, support, or ordain are quickly becoming the basis of the Christian faith. The answer to the question becomes more philosophical if one tries to answer the question with a logical response.

Philosophical in that if one is to say that God changed, with his infinite power and ability, how would one know if He changed? Would God changing, be the course God had already planned or would it be a new course charted by God to redeem himself for some finite purpose. Some will say that God has shown that He will change His mind and there is biblical scripture to support such a position.

While I do not want to expound greatly upon the doctrine of immutability, it would be difficult to show that God has not changed, cannot change and will not change without covering his immutability to some degree. In theology, God's inability to change is known as his immutability. This quality is more easily defined as an inability to change, it is an inability to mutate from one thing to another or one concept to another or one idea to another.

When we discuss the immutability of God, we accept that He is completely incapable of change because to believe that he will change accepts the idea that he is in a way imperfect. Change is brought about to make things perfect that lack perfection, to change a bad decision, or to make something right that somehow went wrong. God's immutability is applied to his character in completeness. That is, every part of Him is perfect and does not require change. The creator does not need to change since He has the ability to change everything else.

To accept the idea that God has changed or changes to accommodate the attitudes and the accepted behavior of men today is to say that He has changed His purpose and His nature to accomplish His will. This inadvertently implies that He did not foreknow the issues that we would face at this time in history. It inadvertently implies that He was inadequately prepared to deal with the issues that face the church at this point in history.

It is a widely misplaced belief that God, in response to prayer, will change His mind to grant the prayers of His believers and His children. While it is true that God answers prayer, it is a mistaken belief that God ever changes His mind or His way to accomplish something for His people. It is more apparent that the people of God, when they are in tune to God, they render prayers that are in line with the perfect will of God. As this occurs, it is the believer that has changed and not God.

God's immutability is essential to our survivability, without it God would be a liar. For those of us that believe in the complete truth of the Bible, there are several scriptures to prove God's immutability. If God were to change, it would mean that He was imperfect and flawed. Other gods have serious and readily apparent flaws. They are flawed in that they all exist only in memory. That is to say, that many of them have lived, died, and had not the power to live again except in the memories or minds of those that believe in them. There is no evidence of any of them rising from the dead. The God of Abraham does not have this flaw, as he is the beginning and the end or the Alpha and Omega.

God clearly tells the Bible reader in Revelation 1:8, 1:11, 21:6 and 22:13, that he is the alpha and omega, the beginning and the end, the first and the last. This is written to show his completeness. For men, our complete life is established by our birth, our life achievements, and our death. God is the beginning of every life, he sustains us throughout our lives, and he is with us when we die. Without his will, nothing would occur. This is what John explained when he wrote: "And this is the confidence we have in him that if we ask anything according to his will, he heareth us" (1 John 5:14). Prayer does not get God to change his will, it allows us to understand his will and see his purpose.

As mentioned above, several scriptures illustrate and verify God's inability to change.

Consider the following scripture:

> "God is not a man, that he should lie; neither the son of man, that he should repent: hath he said, and shall he not do it? or hath he spoke, and shall he not make it good" (Numbers 23:19)?

Malachi 3:6, mentioned earlier, is the definitive biblical proof of God's personal declaration of his immutability. From this scripture, it can be understood that God himself has proclaimed that he does not change. He does not verify this with limitations nor does he decree it as a lack of ability to change.

God's immutability does not have a foundation built upon the principles of inability. The only thing that God is incapable of is lying. This is because of his nature and his power. God is incapable of lying because whatever he says has to happen and whatever he promises he must, because of who he is, fulfill. Many people view their own changes as relating to God having changed. People will, genuinely, believe that God has made them a promise. However, when it does not work out the way that they expected, they tend to say that God has changed his mind. In essence, it is not God that change but the individual. The outcome is different, possibly, for a number of reasons. One is a misinterpretation by the individual. That is, the person did not see, hear, or feel what they thought they did. Another reason could be that the person did not hear from God at all. Another could be that the person did not do all or any of what they were supposed to do. As a result, people try to say that God has changed instead of taking a long hard look at themselves.

As is typical in our society, people do not want to take responsibility for their actions. It occurs in the world and now it is gaining rapid speed and invading the church. People, men and women, will try to justify all that they do by blaming or placing the responsibility on someone else, or in this case saying that God has said something that he has not said. This does not mean that all people try to misrepresent God in their choices: they end up doing so because of outside influences. If no one was around to suggest that I was wrong about something, then I could continue as normal under the thought that I was right. Likewise, if all I had around me were people encouraging me to do what is known to be wrong, until I realize my error, I would continue to walk contrary to what is known or considered right.

Everyone has some justification for doing what he or she does. In times past, people have created what is acceptable within the church by attempting to justify it based upon biblical principles. Homosexuals would have the world believe that the God of Abraham, Isaac and Jacob is now accepting of what he called an abomination in the Bible. The Bible clearly tells those who read it and those who believe it: "If a man also shall lie with mankind, as he lieth with a woman, both of them have committed an abomination: they shall surely be put to death; their blood shall be upon them" (Leviticus 20:13). God has not changed from this view.

The same goes for women that seek the office of pastor. Homosexuals, like women, fail to qualify for the office of pastor even though men in the world put them in the office. Homosexuals, like women, fail to meet the qualification of a "husband of one wife." For if a man would be joined to a man, then who would be the husband or who would be the wife. If people fail to meet the qualifications that God has established, who is man to adjust the qualifications as he may feel appropriate? More importantly, who is man to tell lies on God by saying that God only established those rules for the churches in the Bible when his Word does not support such a view?

It can be said that God allows people to make the right or wrong decision before he does what he already knows that He will do. This does not mean he changes, man makes the changes and God allows for the punishments or the rewards.

If God has not changed and if He is incapable of changing, it is hard to justify that his position with respect to women as pastors has changed. It would be easier to accept that God allows women pastors if there were some biblical evidence proving or illustrating this particular position. However, this burden is not met either as there is no biblical account of a woman pastor or bishop anywhere in the Bible.

No Evidence, No Support For Women Serving As Pastor.

There are no biblical precedents that would suggest that God has changed his mind with regards to the matter of women as pastors. I am one who believes in the whole and completely infallible, inerrant Word of God. However, I do not necessarily agree with the proponents that attempt to use the Old Testament and it's women representatives as proof that God calls women to lead and that in turn means that He calls them to pastor.

It is human nature to want to find justification for what we do, how we may feel, or how we act. Many seek justification when they should look more to taking responsibility. It would be somewhat easy for me to only search for the scriptures or the passages that support the view that God has not made provision for women to be pastors. Yet I find it necessary to look at the people that would be the "supporting cast" for the opposing view. If there is an opposing view, then it must be supported in scripture in some way that clearly places women in the position as pastor. If this is the case, then my position becomes personal and not biblical.

There are several women mentioned in the Bible. Many of them never held a position of authority over men. It would be pointless to give insight into positions held by all of the women mentioned in the Bible. It would be more beneficial to discuss some of the names that many have used to illustrate that women are or can be called to the office of pastor. This is especially true in light of very few scriptures that "clearly" support the practice.

This could be considered a minor study of biblical women that are identified because of some semblance of authority in one position or another and some people who would like to approve of women as pastors use them to argue for women as pastors.

Some scholars provide an account written in the book of 1st Corinthians as grounds for proof of women pastors in the early church. Some would say that Chloe was a church leader because members of her household declared unto Paul that there were contentions among the Corinthians. Paul wrote the following words: "For it hath been declared unto me of you, my brethren, by them which are of the house of Chloe, that there are contentions among you" (1 Corinthians 1:11). This, however, is the only mention of the Chloe in the Bible. In this passage, God makes no mention of Chloe's background or profession, neither is there any reference to her having led a church at her house. Therefore, to say that she was an early pastor is a stretch at best or just plain untrue.

What can be safely concluded, from the passage in Corinthians that introduces Chloe, is that she was, quite possibly, the owner of the house or the head of the household for which people met for church. It is possible that she was a widow; it is also possible that she was divorced. The truth of the matter is that her history was not told in the Bible and very little is known about her outside of the Bible. This does not mean that she was head of the church, led the church, or even preached in the church. It is not even clear from this passage, the only passage that mentions Chloe, whether she sent the members of her household to Paul or whether they went of their own volition. Neither is it clear as to whether the church at Chloe's was excluded from the report to Paul.

There are other problems that would prove to be insurmountable if Chloe is the pastor of the church thought to be in Chloe's house. If Chloe is truly the pastor, I find it a terrible issue that the pastor was unable to deal with these contentions on her own. This is, of course another quality that the pastor should be able to master. In the qualifications for pastors it is written: "For if a man know not how to rule his own house, how shall he take care of the church of God" (1 Timothy 3:5)? From this scripture, it can be seen that the man, that is pastor, should be able to take care of different issues in the church. Again, if Chloe is the pastor, she fails this qualification and it is more believable that she was not the pastor.

In actuality, when one reads the text, it is clear that the people of the house of Chloe were reporting to Paul that there were differences in the teaching that was being done by the teachers and preachers in Corinth. The text reads:

> "Now I beseech you, brethren, by the name of our Lord Jesus Christ, that ye all speak the same thing, and that there be no divisions among you; but that ye be perfectly joined together in the same mind and in the same judgment" (1 Corinthians 1:10).

Presumably, Chloe or others in her house were disturbed by the issues and felt it necessary to warn Paul so that something could be done. This must be because Chloe or the others in the house were unable to influence, correct, or deal with the contentions or the contentious individuals themselves.

People have identified many women in the Bible to try to prove that God has chosen women for positions of leadership. Some of the more notable women that people have identified include

Miriam, Deborah, Priscilla, and Anna. These provide a decent balance of individuals from the Old and New Testaments.

Proponents of this view fail to acknowledge that none of these women held positions of leadership in the church in the Old Testament or in the New Testament. It is chronologically impossible for Old Testament women to be identified or used as evidence of women leaders in the church. This is primarily because they were before Jesus and theirs are not examples of church leadership or pastorship. When discussing pastors of the church, we must understand what church we are actually speaking of and when the church began. Moreover, from the gospel we understand that the church did not begin until after the birth, death, burial, and resurrection of Jesus Christ.

It is necessary to evaluate these women of the Bible, which are used to illustrate God's use of women in leadership, to see if they support the argument for women as pastors. It is not necessary to disprove that these women opened the door for women to be pastor. However, it is necessary to look at their leadership roles and see if the roles and positions they were in provides the evidence that allows for them to be considered pastors.

To gain an understanding of the various women used to illustrate that women are called to lead the church, it is necessary to look at the first mentioned by some. Miriam is one name that I have heard over the years as an example of a woman in the Bible that some profess proves that God will select a woman to lead the church.

> "And MIRIAM the prophetess, the sister of Aaron, took a timbrel in her hand; and all the women went out after her with timbrels and with dances" (Exodus 15:20).

Miriam was called a prophetess in the word of God and the sister of Aaron. Miriam and her brother, at some point, felt that they were just as important to God as Moses was. As a result, they discussed their status as being able to hear from God much like Moses amidst standing against Moses because he had married an Ethiopian woman (see Numbers 12).

As far as her position of leadership goes, Miriam led the women in song, music, and dance following the drowning of the Pharaoh and his men following the Exodus from Egypt. This is what is accounted in Exodus 15:20. As described in the text, Miriam led the women in praise and dance and song.

Miriam was made an example by God in that she became "leprous and white as snow" as punishment for standing up against Moses and having a rebellious discussion with Aaron. In this case, Aaron was not punished as Miriam was punished. In fact, there is no account as to what Aaron's punishment was for his participation in the discussion. It is quite conceivable that Miriam was punished more severely because she was a woman that was a prophetess. On the other hand, it could be that she was punished more severely because she led the discussion or she was the one that started the discussion. If either of these is true, it proves only that she was out of line and out of order leading to her being an example of God's justice for standing against his chosen leader. It is most believable that she orchestrated the discussion and thereby warranted a more severe punishment. Some may say that this is not supported in scripture but it is more clear that it is supported because of the absence of any mention of a punishment for Aaron. In addition, Aaron had to plead for Moses to intervene on Miriam's behalf.

It is understandable that Miriam would be one to lead a small rebellion against Moses as her name is commonly understood to mean "rebellion." Rebels would have no place in the kingdom of God or its operation due to the sheer nature of what they stand for. Rebels are so called because of their nature to stand against authority. Though it need not be discussed again, it is evident and apparent that God does not support nor does He accept rebels.

This may explain why God punished her and not Aaron. Clearly, Miriam makes a poor case for a biblical church leader in that she was a leader against the chosen beloved leader of God in which God was so displeased that he punished her. To say that she is an example for God choosing a woman to lead is a good stretch because other than this account, there is no reference to anything godly that Miriam did nor is there any history of her leading anyone but women.

Miriam is not the only biblical female figure that some scholars attempt to identify as a definitive example of God's desire to use women as individuals to lead the church. Another woman that some have pointed to as a divine appointment that illustrates God's choice of women in leadership is Deborah.

Deborah was also called a prophetess the same as Miriam. However, Deborah was also a judge for Israel during a period when there were no kings and judges ruled. Deborah was a prominent judge for many years. However, her judgeship does not equate to church leadership over men. Her leadership was limited to the individuals that stood before her. While it may be true that she served as judge during a time when judges ruled the nations instead of kings, this does not qualify Deborah as a New Testament pastor. In fact, it would be in poor taste if we were to look at the entire collection of outstanding figures in the Bible and assume that everything they did was done in the will of God.

God made Deborah leader by allowing her to render judgments or have authority over men. However, this is still vastly different from leading the New Testament church. Deborah was a prophetess but she was not a church leader, Pharisee, Sadducee, or even a Priest. Therefore, her position of leadership is not similar to or synonymous with pastoral leadership in any way.

A case could possibly be made that Deborah's position was evidence that God is not a respecter of person or gender when it comes to his chosen leader. In the absence of scripture, that line of thinking would be debatable. For the Bible reader and the Christian's sake, that issue was not left to chance. In this instance, it only provides a general understanding that God allowed women positions of leadership in the world in the Old Testament, New Testament and even today. This still does not provide a decent argument or precedent for God allowing women to pastor the church presently.

There is one named Anna, discussed in Luke 2:36-38. Her story is a beautiful yet brief one. In three verses, the reader is told that she was a prophetess, of the tribe of Aser, the daughter of Phanuel, she lived with her husband for seven years, and that she was a great age. When the reader finds out about her, she is said to be 84 years of age.

The beauty of her story is that she is said to have never left the temple. There is no time given for when she entered the temple, or how long she was there in totality. There is a beauty shown in her commitment to God. She served God through fasting and prayers both day and night. She spent her time telling people about God and she would tell about him to all of the people that looked for redemption in Jerusalem. She in essence and in deed preached to people redemption.

Anna is an excellent example of a woman that preached. She did not preach in hiding, and she was, apparently, not rebuked by the others in the temple. This is evident due to the lack of any account of her having been thrown out of the temple for speaking or preaching and it is evident from the fact that she spent many days, even years doing it.

Some may try to say that this leads to a contradiction of the scriptures because in one instance there is a woman speaking in the temple and in another the Bible says women should keep silent. However, the scriptures are clear and do not provide any contradiction as to the issue of women speaking in church or any other issue. In addition, as the scripture relates to Anna, there can be no question that she was not in violation of 1st Timothy 2:12 because this particular scripture was not a command by God. It should also be kept in mind that Paul's letter to Timothy was written a considerable amount of time later. This could mean several things, but there are two possible understandings that can be reached from this. First, one could believe that many women came behind Anna and began to cause more problems in the church and would not listen to the leaders of the church. Secondly, it could be that the women that followed became uncontrollable in the church.

It is understood from the context of Paul's first letter to the Corinthians, in the 14th chapter, that Paul was addressing issues of chaos that were pervading the church in Corinth. Paul was providing structure and order to the Corinthian church that could be followed today if it were necessary. Most people understand that the churches of God must function in an orderly manner at all times. God does not authorize confusion and church leaders that declare otherwise are in error.

Another woman that has been presented as an example of God using women in positions of leadership is Priscilla and she is another that some identify as proof that God may call women to pastor. Priscilla was the wife of Aquila a Jew born in Pontus. Priscilla is mentioned six times in the Bible. Five times Paul calls her Priscilla and once he calls her Prisca. She and Aquila were privileged to have a house church, which was the church of the day, during the time of their ministry. There are some that assert that by virtue of there being a church in their home, Priscilla served as pastor along with her husband. This is not the nature of things for the time or the church.

Many pastors and teachers have considered the order of naming as an indication of the more prominent person in biblical text. That is, in writing a letter, the name that appeared first is most likely the more prominent figure in the particular text. As such, there are some who say that because Priscilla is mentioned first by Paul in Romans 6:3, she was the more prominent person with regards to her position in the church in their house.

However, when one reads the scriptures identifying Priscilla and Aquila, three times Paul identifies Aquila first (Acts 18:2; 26, 1 Corinthians 16:19) and three times he identifies Priscilla first, (Acts 18:18, Romans 16:3, 1 Timothy 4:19) including the time that he calls Priscilla "Prisca." Based on the above theory, this makes identifying the one that Paul considered more prominent difficult. However, Paul was one that believed that man was the head so it is inconceivable that he would disrespect Aquila by placing his wife ahead of him and the leader over him. If we are to understand that the Bible is inerrant and infallible, we must understand that God has not placed any contradictions in the Bible to confuse the people. This is another, unfortunate attempt by some to open a closed door to allow a way for something that God is against to enter into the minds of the Christian.

Furthermore, most of Paul's letters began with him identifying himself first. Under the premise of first named, he should be the more prominent figure in all of the texts he wrote. Paul wrote many acknowledgements to those who helped further the gospel with him. I believe that the order of naming was not as prominent an issue as some would like. After all, the words were still inspired by God.

It is clear from the scriptures that Priscilla, cooperated with her husband in teaching and speaking the word of God. The

Bible says nothing against the private witnessing of women or the public witnessing of women for that matter. Women may show the lost the way of salvation, or they may witness to those who believe so that others may understand the word more perfectly as Priscilla did with her husband in Acts 18:26.

Clearly, Priscilla is another good example of a woman that preached but she still fails to make the case for a woman being pastor. In fact the key to the matter is that much of Priscilla's work was acknowledged by Paul prior to him admonishing and correcting the Corinthian church and instructing Timothy. This does not mean nor does it show that Paul was accepting of a woman as pastor, as some would have us to believe. It is a more feasible conclusion that this illustrates that Paul was accepting of women as preachers. This is the only reasonable conclusion since Paul was clearly against women as pastors or bishops. This is also a more reasonable conclusion since it was Paul who penned the hierarchy in the family of God, telling us all that man is at the head of woman.

After all of this, there are some who would attempt to use Galatians 3:28 as another text that may help them prove that God can and will call women to pastor. The scripture reads:

> "There is neither Jew nor Greek, there is neither bond nor free, there is neither male nor female: for ye are all one in Christ Jesus" (Galatians 3:28.)

In the letter to the Galatians, Paul admonished the Galatians for their not having understood that their receiving of the Holy Spirit was not by the law but by hearing the faith. He explains to them that they were redeemed from the law by Christ. After all of this and much more, he comes to conclude with verse 28. In it, Paul explains that all are on equal ground and all receive the same gift in Christ. Yet it still does not mean that women are to be pastors. In the Bible, today's reader is not dealing with the law of man; they are dealing with the precepts of God. Nowhere does Paul discount any of the other letters that he wrote, nor does he nullify or revoke anything he wrote to Timothy.

For people to say that verse 28 opens this door they would also have to agree that, according to this scripture, any person could be pastor. This would include persons that were not sober, had more than one wife, had bad behavior, fighters, covetors, alcoholics, etc. If all were equal, as stated in Galatians 3:28 under the premise that individuals use for women pastors, then the preceding statement would have to be true as well. Those of us who do not wish to pervert the word of God understand that this is not the case here.

Furthermore, if the biblical qualifications for pastors does not apply to women, then does that mean that they can be fighters, alcoholics, have unruly children, etc? If the qualifications do not apply then what rules or guides the woman pastor? Do all of the other scriptures in 1 Timothy apply except for the verse that says "husband?"

Could They Be Mistaken?

It is possible and people must realize that they could be misled in their belief. For that matter, even I could be misled. However, I know without a doubt that the Bible is right. People, Christians in particular, must realize that the devil is capable of great deception. The devil's power of deception is evidenced in his temptation of Jesus Christ in the wilderness.

> "and the devil, taking him up into and high mountain, showed unto him all the kingdoms of the world in a moment of time. And the devil said unto him, all this power will I give thee and the glory of them: for that is delivered unto me; and to whomsoever 1 will give it" (Luke 4:5-6).

In this temptation, Jesus does not deny that the devil had power, neither did he rebuke the devil for using his power. Though the devil may not have had the power to give all that he showed to Jesus, it is clear that it was by the devil's power that it was shown to him. Now for understanding, all must realize that God gives all power and so are the rights to use any power that God has given.

From the temptation of Jesus, one can see that the devil has power to show people things, to tempt people, and to mislead people and even the power to carry them to something. However, he does not have power over people as some would believe. The devil can only do what one would allow whether it is God or the individual. If it were not so then all people would have been possessed, as some in the Bible were possessed. This would be the devil's tactic and if you think about it, it would be a winning tactic because everyone would be on his side.

By understanding that the devil has power and is capable of great deception, we are better able to evaluate our decisions. When looking at the subject of pastors and preachers, the Bible gives us great foundation on the subject. We have the biblical qualifications for pastors (bishops) in 1st Timothy. However, we have much more than that when it comes to scripture. In the book of Romans we find these words:

> "How then shall they call on him in whom they have not believed? and how shall they believe in him of whom they have not heard? and how shall they hear without a preacher? And how shall they preach, except they be sent? as it is written, How beautiful are the feet of them that preach the gospel of peace, and bring glad tidings of good things" (Romans 10:14,15)!

In the passage in Romans 10:14-15 it is clear that true preachers will be sent by God. This does not mean some people will not go of their own desire or that some will not be sent by the devil. From other scriptures, we are informed that there will be many false prophets and teachers. In fact, in his teaching on false witnesses, Jesus gives us the following words:

> "Beware of false prophets, which come to you in sheep's clothing, but inwardly they are ravening wolves. Ye shall know them by their fruits. Do men gather grapes of thorns, or figs of thistles? Even so every good tree bringeth forth good fruit; but a corrupt tree bringeth forth evil fruit. A good tree cannot bring forth evil fruit, neither

can a corrupt tree bring forth good fruit. Every tree that bringeth not forth good fruit is hewn down, and cast into the fire. Wherefore by their fruits ye shall know them" (Matthew 7:15-20).

Jesus, in this passage, illustrates that there will be false witnesses or prophets to look out for and what believers must look for are their fruit. We should not look at their posture, their assets, their gender or even their stature. We must look for their fruit. Many people do not know what fruit we are to look for, but the Bible is specific in what fruit true Christians should bear. If we did not know what they were, we could be fooled or led astray by false witnesses, false teachers, false prophets, and even non-believers.

In Galatians 5:19-23 we can gain an understanding of the works of the flesh and the fruit of the Spirit.

"Now the works of the flesh are manifest, which are these; Adultery, fornication, uncleanness, lasciviousness, Idolatry, witchcraft, hatred, variance, emulations, wrath, strife, seditions, heresies, Envyings, murders, drunkenness, revellings, and such like: of the which I tell you before, as I have also told you in time past, that they which do such things shall not inherit the kingdom of God. But the fruit of the Spirit is love, joy, peace, longsuffering, gentleness, goodness, faith, Meekness, temperance: against such there is no law" (Galatians 5:19-23).

Two of the attributes of the works of the flesh are strife which is more easily understood as self-ambition, and sedition which is more easily understood as dissensions. These are important in this discussion because, I believe, that self-ambition leads people to disregard the word of God in whatever instance they see fit. In this case, it causes people to disregard what God has set aside for men or husbands to allow women or wives. In addition, self-ambition is what I believe causes some people to desire the office of pastor. Men and women sometimes take the office of pastor under false pretenses to further exalt himself or herself or grow in their own minds.

As it is written in the biblical qualifications for bishops, the man that desires the office of bishop should not be greedy for filthy lucre. This greed is what, I believe, leads some people to take the office of pastor. As it is written in Romans, preachers will be sent. I believe that some men have come to think that they have been charged with sending God's preachers here and there, but they will be sent by God and not by man. Some denominations appoint pastors to different churches to fill vacancies that may be present. I know that sometimes those appointments are not based on spiritual grounds. Sometimes the appointee is moved around as punishment for one thing or another. Men send men for their own purposes, God sends men for his purposes.

Dissension can be understood as having a difference of opinion. In this discussion, people's dissension comes into play because their opinion differs from that of God. That is, people are saying that God has changed or God did not mean what is written in the Bible the way it has been interpreted. It appears to me that people think that God is somehow different or was somehow confused, they do what they will and still claim to be operating in the name of God. This is no different than a psychic reading futures for people and proclaiming God at the same time. Self-ambition and dissension are key works of the flesh. Most can agree that the flesh is powerful in persuading an individual to do different things. Jesus explained: "Watch and pray, that ye enter not into temptation: the spirit indeed is willing, but the flesh is weak" (Matthew 26:41). When He explains that the flesh is weak, it is in obvious comparison to the spirit. In this statement, the temptation is more an issue for the flesh than it is for the spirit. This may explain why there are so many more men and women doing what they feel to be okay or right as opposed to what is known or written to be right.

Self-ambition could also be understood as an issue that comes out of pride. Self-ambition is something that conflicts with a leader's ambitions. A leader's ambition is, basically, the leader's desire or their will. All believers should keep this in mind when we work in the church. We should put our own personal ambitions aside in favor of the leader's ambitions. God is the leader and if we fall in line with His will and His desire, then we will be successful in everything we try. Failure to follow the leader puts us in a position where we can be misled or mistaken in things that we do.

The spiritual fruit (fruit of the spirit) has not changed from when it was first written to us in the Bible. What all must understand is that God has not changed his mind about his word to suit any purpose. All believers, especially prophets, preachers and teachers must bear these fruit. No mistake can be made in what the people of God should look for in others that preach and teach the Word of God.

Whose Appointment Is Most Important?

"For I say, through the grace given unto me, to every man that is among you, not to think of himself more highly THAN HE OUGHT to think; but to think soberly, according as God hath dealt to every man the measure of faith" (Romans 12:3).

It may be true that men have relinquished their authority in their homes and in their churches to women but this does not mean that God recognizes that relinquished power or that God recognizes the one who holds a position outside of who God has appointed. God's appointments are more important than man's appointments as evidenced in the way that God dealt with Korah and his fellow rebels following their attempt to take power or duties from Moses because they felt that they were just as capable as Moses and Aaron. Korah's fall was recorded in the book of Numbers.

"And they gathered themselves together against Moses and against Aaron, and said unto them, [Ye take] too much upon you, seeing all the congregation [are] holy, every one of them, and the LORD [is] among them: wherefore then lift ye up yourselves above the congregation of the LORD" (Numbers 16:2)?

In the above verse, Korah and those that were willing to follow his lead believes more in himself than he should and he believes that God sees him in the same way that he sees Moses, his chosen one. Korah, like many people today, was wrong. It is not up to man or woman to decide where they stand with God; it is a divine appointment solely (see Jeremiah 1:5).

When one takes on more than one has been given, one will oftentimes take on their own damnation. If a person decides that they can do the same as or better than the one that God has appointed, then that person crosses a line that God has established. This is what the problem became for the sons of Levi.

> "And put fire therein, and put incense in them before the LORD to morrow: and it shall be [that] the man whom the LORD doth choose, he [shall be] holy: [ye take] too much upon you, ye sons of Levi" (Numbers 16:7).

Korah and his followers did as Moses had said and found that they were not God's choice and they were punished for their rebellion. Moses did not relinquish his God given power to Korah but allowed Korah to stand before and to be judged by God. The word of God is consistent in that individuals that try to take on more than they have been given are punished. It does not matter whether the position they take on is by endorsement or personal belief. Korah and the others had a personal belief that God would recognize them as his chosen leaders yet they found out otherwise.

The church must understand that relinquished power does not translate into recognized power. All power is given by God. As you read the Bible, you will come to find that even the devil has power. To see more of his power, one just needs to look at what he did to Job. Satan spoke to God saying, "Hast not thou made an hedge about him, and about his house, and about all that he hath on every side? thou hast blessed the work of his hands, and his substance is increased in the land. But put forth thine hand now, and touch all that he hath, and he will curse thee to thy face. And the LORD said unto Satan, Behold, all that he hath [is] in thy power; only upon himself put not forth thine hand"(Job 1:10-12a).

From this scripture, we can easily see that Satan was given the right to use his power on all that Job had. What is wonderful to see, is that God did not give Satan power over Job just over all that he had. God still has not changed. God provided the rules and laws for us to go by but he has not given man the power or authority to disregard those rules as he feels the need to do. Neither has God given man the right to transfer his power to anyone else. The acceptance of women as pastors, to me, is no different (in essence) than a professed homosexual taking the pulpit to preach and proclaiming to follow the whole Bible. Both are going against the will of God and both are out of order.

I understand that some people will try to say that many preachers, pastors, and ministers sin. This is obviously a true statement and it is undeniable. There is no need to try to support or abase any of those ideas. It is also true that sin is sin and there are no big sins or little sins. One either does what is asked or does not do what is asked. What can be said is that most preachers, ministers, and pastors do not flaunt or advertise their sin. Committing sin is one thing but flaunting it would be twice as bad because it completely contradicts the gospel or message that one professes to embrace. At the core and in light of knowing what the scriptures teach, to hold a position in a way that contradicts the scriptures would be flaunting flagrant disagreement with the word of God and shows unbelief.

It is clear that no man or woman's words are greater than the word of God. So it does not matter how prominent the preacher or pastor is, it does not matter how famous they are, it does not matter how many books they have written or songs that they sing, if what they/we do does not stand in equality to the word of God we are all out of order. This is true in all spiritual and functional matters of the church.

If a pastor says that God's word does not exclude women from occupying the office of pastor, either they have not studied the scriptures or they do not agree with them. This leads to true rebellion, which God has identified as a sin. There is a difference when someone does something and does not know it is wrong and when they do something but know that it is wrong. That is to say, that pastors and preachers that do not know what the scriptures say about their office are wrong in that they have not studied the scriptures or searched them to determine their own validity.

If someone in the faith were to tell me there is something that I should or should not be doing in ministry, I evaluate their words by what the scriptures say. If there is some validity in the scriptures then I may or may not follow their advice. If there is no justification in the scriptures then I, most definitely, will not do what they suggest. I never have and prayerfully never will fall into that trap which can so easily be set for any of the children of God.

For instance, I know that Jesus was the last sacrifice that God required for the remission of man's sin. Knowing this truth, if someone of the faith was to tell me that I needed to start sacrificing animals to please God, I am definitely going to search the scriptures to keep from doing something that God has not ordained.

In the book of Daniel, Daniel informed king Nebuchadnezzar of God's authority as it relates to his power of appointment.

> "Daniel answered and said, Blessed be the name of God forever and ever: for wisdom and might are his: And he

changeth the times and the seasons: he removeth kings, and setteth up kings: he giveth wisdom unto the wise, and knowledge to them that know understanding:" (Daniel 2:20-21).

Daniel is letting the king know that he did not set himself up as king and neither did any other man set him up as king. No man has the power to set in place something so spectacular. Mankind can only do what God allows him or her to do. Furthermore, just because God allows it, does not means that he approves of it. In our recent history, it has been said that the 43rd President of the United States somehow, some way stole the presidential election in the year 2000. Whether it was stolen or not, it was God's will and for his purpose. It does not take a rocket scientist to see the problems that have occurred in the world during that particular president's tenure in office. Regardless of the reason or purposes behind that president being in office, it was the will of God.

It proves that God sets up leaders and he has a way of taking them down. In the case of Nebuchadnezzar and the 43rd president of the United States, they were both allowed to serve and seemingly, both served their own purpose instead of God's. The king was taken down and set out by God because of his own pride. This president will be more remembered for the bad things and missteps he made than for anything good that he may have done.

What does it Hurt?

I will admit that there are many charismatic, persuasive, knowledgeable, understanding, eloquent, ideological, personable, and challenging women that are capable of leading God's church. If qualities were all that were necessary to be pastor then there are many people that may fit the mold of being pastor. Unfortunately being pastor does not come down to qualities but qualifications. The qualifications brought out in 1 Timothy 3 and Titus 1 are, without question, clear written evidence of what God's choice for leading his church on earth is and should be. Unfortunately, as pressured by the world, the church has begun to turn from obeying the word of God in favor of gaining more acceptance in the world. That is, we are in the midst of an age to whereby the thought is anything goes and thus anything should be accepted.

We live in a society in which most people detest labels and stereotypes. The same feelings have moved into the church where people would like for their imperfections to be accepted without challenge. It is 100 percent true that the Lord loves His children. It is also true that God is against sin. We are 100 percent imperfect beings but we are not saved to perfection. We are saved because we desire perfection and salvation. Even the consummate perfectionist that you may know has to at some point in their life deal with his or her own imperfection. In fact, I make the case that most people are perfectionists as a way of dealing with their own imperfections.

Unfortunately, the same people that have a great aversion to stereotypes, name-calling and degradation of others revert to such tactics when they find one with beliefs contrary to their own. My purpose is not to divide, or divert people's attention from the usefulness of women in the ministry of the gospel. Their usefulness is undeniable, their messages can be sound and solid but the methods must be as just as the word that they preach. This is true of all ministers of the gospel, which makes it true for all believers. All believers have been commissioned to obey the Word of God and teach others the same message.

Whether people believe in it or not, there is a clergy class as related to the work of kingdom building. There is also such a thing as kingdom building. Adding to the body of Christ, adds to the kingdom of God provided the additions perform as we have been commanded. It does not matter what religion we claim to be a part of, if leaders claim to use the Bible as the foundational basis for their biblical doctrine, the words "husband of one wife" are undeniable.

It is undeniable that there are many female figures in the Bible. They fail to provide definitive proof to support women being called by God to lead his church. There may be plenty of conjecture, and expostulation but our answers should come from the word of God that we love so much. God has given men the ability to lead the church and to do so as he has designed. This does not mean that women are incapable of leading God's church; it just means that the position has not been designed, created, or ordained for them. Much like the position of father has not been designed for them or the position of mother being designed for a man. Obviously, there are good reasons for God not designing the position of pastor for women. Several of them have been discussed and outlined in the Bible (weaker vessel, first deceived, feeble, etc.)

What must be kept at the forefront for the direction of the church is the order of the institution and order in the institution.

Godly women should be subject to their husbands as outlined in Ephesians 5:23-24, unfortunately women have found it difficult in coming to terms with the term "subject." Most people, men and women, especially in the United States, have been trained or conditioned to understand that they have a voice that is worthy of being heard. Many people have gathered to their belief system that subjection implies inferiority in some way. People are reluctant to give up their freewill and many feel that it is given up if they succumb to the trap of being considered less than someone else. This is an untrue assessment and a poor attempt by many to maintain a sense of authority in areas where it has not been granted. If we look at the concept of subjection, it applies to all. Every person in every situation is subject to someone or something else at any given moment. Those who accept those things to which they are subject tend to have more pleasant experiences than those who do not.

Subjection is not oppression. Jesus Christ does not oppress the church nor does he burden us with a forceful hand, instead He asks the church to perform as expected. It seems as though people are moved to be on the defensive when told that they are subject to another. It has been said several different ways, but it all comes down to people, men and women all at one point or another in their everyday lives, want to be the leader more than they want to be led.

Men are not to use subjection as a tool to justify mistreatment of the wife. In fact the Bible tells men to love their wives in the way that Christ loved the church (see Ephesians 5:25). How did Christ love the church? He died for the church.

Who is man to know why God has established the order in the way he has, except it is revealed to man from God himself? There are no new revelations being provided to men or women nor are there any changes to what he has already said. We have been given the prophecy concerning the future of this world and the end of times. We have been told of God's desire for all of humanity and we know that the Messiah shall return. The word of God is complete and no man, save God or Jesus himself, can add to it or take away from it. Even our most spirit-filled church leaders are not being given inspiration that will contradict or overturn what God has given to us. If any claim to receive such, they are false prophets of whom Jesus warned us. God has established the order and has identified it thoroughly throughout the Bible to guide his people in the direction for his church.

An in-depth study of the scriptures will reveal that the man and the woman, at some point, shared some equality in the eyes of the Lord while still in the garden. This is easy to see from what God told Eve after the fall as he sentenced her for her role in the disobedience to His command. There is no mention as to the status of man and woman in relation to each other's stature, prior to God punishments. Nevertheless, He gave the following words to the woman in Genesis 3:16: "Unto the woman he said, I will greatly multiply thy sorrow and thy conception; in sorrow thou shall bring forth children; and thy desire [shall be] to thy husband, and he shall rule over thee." From this point on Eve, and women that would follow her, was subjected to being ruled over by man. This does not provide authority to man to exert undue power over women but the husband is always in front of or above the woman through the eyes of God. The good man knows that any damage he causes to his wife, he indeed causes to himself whether it be physical, emotional, or otherwise.

However, being subject to subjection does not open the door for women to avoid marriage or even seek divorce to be able to pastor churches. It has been established that women are to not occupy the office of pastor under any circumstance. Some have theorized elaborate loopholes where it may be necessary for women to lead. One of the most far-reaching theories would be if all of the men in the world were somehow eliminated or were not willing to serve God in the pastoral capacity. With the prophet Jonah, the Bible scholar can see that God has many ways, at his disposal, to persuade his prophet, his preacher and his pastor to do his will. Therefore, there is no chance that none of the men that God has chosen will do his will. Remember, God knew all of us before we were conceived and he chose his leaders before they were in the womb (see Jeremiah 1:5).

The understanding of who may not be pastor includes those women that would sit as co-pastors. I understand that those that sit as co-pastors are not "necessarily" the pastor of the church. However, what becomes the role of the co-pastor in the event something happens to the pastor? Is it not by design that the co-pastor becomes the pastor in the event that something happens to the pastor? Many understand that in an aircraft there is, generally, a pilot and a co-pilot. The co-pilot mostly operates to assist the pilot in operating the craft. However, in the event that something happens to the pilot, then the co-pilot becomes the one in charge of the craft. If this is not the intention of the pastors that have such an arrangement then it may be necessary to change what we call our wives that operate in the ministry with us.

If pastors are making their wives co-pastors to show unity of the word, it is wrong. Presently, I understand that my wife has not been called into the ministry to preach. I would be wrong to set her up as a preacher or co-pastor. Likewise, I would be wrong to put that pressure on her to preach or co-pastor when this is not what God has called her to do.

This book has not been produced to alienate, defame, belittle or even discount my sisters in the ministry of the gospel.

However, we must be truthful in our carrying out the work of the Lord as we are all charged to do. There is no discount for sin, which is working outside of the will of God. We must serve the Lord and follow his commandments. This would include every command regardless of how we may feel about the command. The testimony of the true believer is that they keep all of the commandments of God. Ultimately, this means that one should bring oneself into subjection to God and to those that He has put in authority over us.

There are several scriptures throughout the Bible, which God has commanded us to keep his commandments. In the New Testament alone we find the following scriptures:

> "And hereby we do know that we know him, if we keep his commandments" (1 John 2:3).
>
> "And whatsoever we ask, we receive of him, because we keep his commandments, and do those things that are pleasing in his sight" (1 John 3:22).
>
> "And he that keepeth his commandments dwelleth in him, and he in him.
>
> And hereby we know that he abideth in us, by the Spirit which he hath given us" (I John 3:24).
>
> "By this we know that we love the children of God, when we love God, and keep his commandments" (1 John 5:2).
>
> "For this is the love of God, that we keep his commandments: and his commandments are not grievous" (1 John 5:3).

His command, concerning pastors, is that a bishop (pastor) must be the husband of one wife. This should remove any ambiguity that may exist on the subject yet we still have the issues that have begun to gain momentum in our churches. God has not established his rules to bind us or hurt us but he has established them for us to lead the world back to him. It is difficult, at best, for the church to lead people to God when the world sees that we do not completely follow His will, His way or His commandments. This, in essence, tells the world that we serve a God that is okay with some defiance from his followers when He truly is not okay with it at all.

We must beware of all who do not want to embrace the word and will of God. His Love is great and his power is mighty. No preacher or believer is excluded from having to submit to the word and the will of God. The choice to submit and obey God is the responsibility of each individual and each individual will have to give an account when it comes time to be judged. God does not show in his word that he will discount a person's sin because they led many people to him. On the contrary, Jesus explained in Matthew 7:23-24 that many who profess to save many and cast out devils will be turn away in the Day of Judgment. Do we not preach that those who hear turn away from their sinful ways whereby they can avoid being turned away?

Some proponents would have the church to think that there is some sort of conspiracy, by men of the church and ignorant women in the church, to oppress or keep other women under some sort of unwritten form of bondage. As has been shown throughout this book, men that do not allow women to pastor, have a firm biblical footing to sustain their position. It is entirely possible that some are chauvinist. It is also entirely possible that some have other issues with women. However, even if some of these may be true, it does not limit the power of the Word of God. In truth, whatever their worldly beliefs may be, they are justified by the word to not ordain women pastors and, in some cases, they may even be justified by the word to not allow women to preach. That, in my view, has to be between them and the Lord. As seen in this book, Paul provided a foundation that illustrates that the pastor must do what is best for the service of God and the delivery of the message.

I believe that those women who are currently out of order run the risk of standing before Jesus and being one of those that he says "depart from me." However, this is only a risk if they choose to remain out of order. People must understand that there is no shame in repentance it only brings us closer to salvation. Pride and arrogance may keep some women on the outside of God's will but true believers will turn and change to be in line with the word and will of God. The goal of all preachers and pastors should be to unify the church and lead people to God. This goal is not by any means necessary but by the ways and the will of God. We should not resort to breaking God's rules to say that we serve his purpose but we should follow his commandments to fulfill his word.

God has not ordained women occupying the office of pastor nor has He accepted it. It has been allowed by men and in some cases commandeered by women. Good intentions do not lead to forgiveness. God is our ultimate judge and what we will be judged on will be what we have done to and for others and whether we have followed his commandments in doing those things.

Some women will say that they cannot be wrong because they are doing good or great things and they are doing what the Lord has called all men and women to do. It is true that we are all called to do different things. However, we are all called to do them in order. Men are to be in subjection to Christ and women are to be in subjection to men. Man cannot be above Christ and women cannot be above men. Men cannot lead Christ and therefore women cannot be in the lead of men in the church. Others might say that their church is mostly women. To that, it can be said that mostly does not mean all. Furthermore, going around a barrier, does not mean that the barrier is no longer there, it just means that one was able to get around it. Does that mean that breaking the law is okay as long as we can get around it? The answer is surely no. Finding a way around the scriptures is just as wrong for anyone that does it.

It is clear that being out of order is not looked at, by God, as a good or noble thing. As He illustrated to us in His punishment of Korah, He is not accepting of disorder or self-made leaders. It is also clear that purposefully going against the Word of God will have severe consequences. God has clearly shown us that He will punish accordingly and rightfully. Through love, God sent His soon to redeem the world, in love I write this book and it should be in live that people that are out of order step aside and assume their rightful positions in the church, wherever that may be. By the Word of God, we know that it is not as pastor or deacon in the church dedicated to serving the Lord.

If it were man's decision as to who could and could not lead the church of God, I must admit that there would be no reason for me to write this book outside of worldly influences. I have seen, met and even interacted with several women who I believe are capable of leading a church. I have been impressed and yes even inspired by a number of women who I believe could pastor a church. Nevertheless, one of the important things to remember is that this is one of those decisions that is not mandated by man. God has not implied nor has he explicitly said that the church should choose its pastor from any living being in the church. He has established a criteria and a method to finding and selecting his pastors. The church, the body of Christ must embrace the Lord's methods and understand that going around them does not help the church or the body. It does not help the one going around those methods either.

We must not be defensive, hateful or even hurt by having the truth revealed. We must be sincere, loving, and maintain order to lead unbelievers to Christ and keep believers encouraged. The leadership in the church must not be the source of disorder or corruption in the church. The word of God gives us the following words:

> "Get wisdom, get understanding: forget it not; neither decline from the words of my mouth. Forsake her not, and she shall preserve thee: love her, and she shall keep thee. Wisdom is the principal thing; therefore get wisdom: and with all thy getting get understanding" (Proverbs 4:5-7).

Wisdom allows us to make sense of and use what we know, what we know is the basis of what we understand. Know that God loves us all; understand that His love will not replace His judgments. Understand that as advocate, Jesus has decreed what His judgment will be for those who do not cast out devils, save the lost and heal the sick as the Lord has given us power to do. Operating outside of our area will not gain any of us additional points with God in that day.